The Cross-Platform Code Revolution

Building Scalable, Secure, and Agile Applications with Python, C#, and .NET Core

THOMPSON CARTER

Table of Content

TABLE OF CONTENTS

11

Introduction

MASTERING CROSS-PLATFORM DEVELOPMENT WITH PYTHON, C#, AND .NET CORE

In today's fast-paced software development world, building applications that work seamlessly across multiple platforms—whether it's on mobile devices, desktops, or web browsers—has become an essential skill for developers. Whether you're developing for **iOS**, **Android**, **Windows**, **macOS**, or the **cloud**, ensuring that your application runs smoothly on all of them is no longer a luxury but a necessity. This book is your comprehensive guide to mastering the art and science of **cross-platform development** using **Python**, **C#**, and **.NET Core**.

With the ever-growing demand for applications that work seamlessly across different devices and operating systems, the traditional approach of developing for a single platform has become inefficient. Today, cross-platform development is the key to delivering quality, high-performance software that reaches a broader audience. This book aims to equip you with the tools, techniques, and best practices needed to create efficient, scalable, and maintainable cross-platform applications, regardless of the platform or environment.

Why Cross-Platform Development?

Cross-platform development allows you to write your code once and deploy it to multiple platforms. This approach saves both time and resources by enabling developers to maintain a single codebase that can be compiled and executed on **Android, iOS, Windows, macOS**, and even in the cloud. With cross-platform tools, developers can avoid the challenges of building separate native apps for each platform, reducing the cost of development and maintenance.

Cross-platform technologies have evolved significantly in recent years, making it easier for developers to create **high-performance applications** with **native experiences** across all platforms. Frameworks and tools like **.NET MAUI, Xamarin, Flutter, React Native, Kivy**, and **Blazor** have changed the game, allowing you to focus on solving business problems instead of worrying about platform-specific limitations.

In this book, we focus on two **powerhouse technologies—Python** and **C#** with **.NET Core**—to guide you through the essential steps of creating cross-platform applications. Whether you're building mobile apps, web apps, or even working with IoT devices, **Python** and **C#** will allow you to build robust, scalable, and future-proof solutions for any platform.

What You'll Learn

This book is divided into **20 chapters**, each designed to introduce you to key concepts and practical tools needed for successful cross-platform development. Whether you're a beginner or an experienced developer, you'll find insights and hands-on examples that will elevate your understanding of cross-platform application development. Here's what you can expect to learn:

- **Foundations of Cross-Platform Development**: Learn why cross-platform development is essential, and how Python and C# with .NET Core are at the forefront of this evolution.
- **Choosing the Right Tech Stack**: Understand when to use **Python** vs. **C#** and how .NET Core fits into the cross-platform development landscape.

- **Building Cross-Platform UI**: Explore how to create rich user interfaces using **WPF**, **MAUI**, and **Blazor** in .NET, or **Kivy** and **PyQt** in Python.

- **Mobile Development**: Dive into building mobile applications using **Xamarin**, **.NET MAUI**, and **Kivy**. Learn how to develop apps that run seamlessly on **Android** and **iOS** with a single codebase.

- **Blockchain & IoT Integration**: Learn how to integrate **blockchain technology** and create **IoT applications** using Python and .NET Core, from building decentralized apps (DApps) to connecting **Raspberry Pi** and **Arduino** devices.

- **AI and Machine Learning**: See how to integrate **AI** and **machine learning** into cross-platform apps, with practical examples using Python's **TensorFlow** and **Scikit-learn**, as well as **ML.NET** in C#.

- **CI/CD for Cross-Platform Deployment**: Automate your workflows with **CI/CD** pipelines using **GitHub Actions** and **Azure DevOps** to deploy apps across all platforms, from **mobile** to **desktop** and **cloud**.

- **Security, Scalability, and Performance**: Understand how to build secure, scalable, and high-performance apps, with best practices for **authentication**, **authorization**, and **performance profiling**.

- **The Future of Cross-Platform Development**: Explore where the industry is headed, including the role of **5G**,

edge computing, **WebAssembly**, and emerging tools in the cross-platform development space.

Why This Book Is For You

Whether you're a seasoned developer or someone new to cross-platform development, this book is designed to provide you with everything you need to create **high-quality, efficient, and scalable cross-platform applications**.

- **Python Developers**: You'll learn how to leverage your Python knowledge to build mobile, desktop, web, and even **IoT applications**, using frameworks like **Kivy**, **Flask**, **Django**, and **PyQt**.
- **C#/.NET Developers**: You'll get a deep dive into **.NET Core**, **Xamarin**, **.NET MAUI**, and **Blazor**, with practical examples on creating **mobile apps**, **web apps**, and **desktop apps**.
- **Beginners**: If you're just starting your journey in cross-platform development, this book will provide you with a solid foundation, step-by-step tutorials, and practical exercises to build real-world applications.
- **Experienced Developers**: For those familiar with Python or .NET, this book will provide valuable insights into advanced topics such as **blockchain integration**, **AI** and

machine learning, and **security** practices for developing enterprise-level cross-platform applications.

What Sets This Book Apart?

- **Hands-on Approach**: Every chapter is filled with **real-world examples** and code snippets to help you apply what you've learned immediately.
- **Balanced Focus on Python and C#**: This book equally covers both **Python** and **C#** for cross-platform development, so whether you're a Pythonista or a .NET developer, you'll find plenty of useful content.
- **Diverse Application Examples**: You won't just learn how to build basic apps; you'll also explore advanced use cases such as **blockchain development, IoT integration**, and **machine learning**, ensuring that you're ready for the future of cross-platform development.

The Future Is Cross-Platform

Cross-platform development is no longer a trend; it's the future of application development. Whether you're building apps for **mobile**, **desktop**, **cloud**, or **IoT**, this book will provide you with the tools, knowledge, and confidence to succeed in this fast-moving landscape. As technology continues to evolve, the ability to write apps that work across **different devices and platforms** will be one of the most valuable skills in the tech world.

Let's dive in, and explore the endless possibilities that **Python** and **C#/.NET Core** offer for building the next generation of **cross-platform applications**.

PART 1

FOUNDATIONS OF CROSS-PLATFORM DEVELOPMENT

CHAPTER 1

INTRODUCTION TO CROSS-PLATFORM DEVELOPMENT

Why Cross-Platform Coding Matters

In today's software landscape, developers need to build applications that **work seamlessly across multiple platforms**—Windows, macOS, Linux, Android, iOS, and even web environments. Gone are the days when developers wrote separate codebases for different platforms. Instead, cross-platform development **saves time, reduces costs, and ensures a consistent user experience.**

The Evolution of Cross-Platform Development

- In the early days of computing, applications were built specifically for one platform (e.g., Windows apps using C++ or .NET Framework, macOS apps using Objective-C).
- The rise of **Java** introduced the **"Write Once, Run Anywhere"** philosophy, but it wasn't perfect.

- **Frameworks like .NET Core, Python, Xamarin, and Blazor** have transformed cross-platform development, allowing developers to write a single codebase that runs across multiple environments.

Cross-platform coding isn't just a convenience—it's a necessity for modern businesses and developers looking to maximize their reach.

The Benefits of Using Python, C#, and .NET Core

Each programming language and framework brings unique advantages to cross-platform development.

Python: Simplicity and Versatility

- Python is known for its **easy-to-read syntax**, making it accessible to beginners and powerful for experienced developers.
- It's widely used in **web development, automation, data science, AI, and scripting.**
- Python's cross-platform capabilities allow developers to **write code once and execute it on Windows, macOS, and Linux without modification.**

C#: High Performance and Enterprise-Grade Development

- C# is a **strongly typed, object-oriented** language designed for building high-performance applications.
- With **.NET Core**, C# applications run efficiently on multiple platforms.
- It's ideal for **desktop applications, game development (Unity), and enterprise solutions.**

.NET Core: The Future of Microsoft Development

- .NET Core is an **open-source, cross-platform framework** that supports building apps for **Windows, Linux, and macOS**.
- It's designed for **modern cloud applications, microservices, and high-performance systems.**
- Developers can use **Blazor, .NET MAUI, and ASP.NET Core** to build **desktop, mobile, and web applications with a single codebase.**

Common Myths and Misconceptions

Despite its benefits, cross-platform development has faced skepticism. Let's debunk some common myths.

Myth 1: Cross-Platform Apps Are Slower Than Native Apps

Reality: Modern frameworks like .NET Core and optimized Python runtimes offer near-native performance. With **JIT (Just-in-Time) compilation and AOT (Ahead-of-Time) optimizations**, apps run efficiently across platforms.

Myth 2: You Must Sacrifice UI/UX for Cross-Platform Development

Reality: Frameworks like **.NET MAUI, Blazor, and PyQt** allow developers to create **beautiful, native-like interfaces** while keeping the codebase unified.

Myth 3: Cross-Platform Development is Only for Web Apps

Reality: While web apps benefit significantly from cross-platform strategies, **desktop (WPF, .NET MAUI), mobile (Xamarin, Flutter), and even AI-powered applications** can be built using Python and C#.

Myth 4: Cross-Platform Development is Hard to Maintain

Reality: Using modern development practices like **modular code design, microservices, and API-driven architectures** makes maintenance just as easy as traditional development.

Final Thoughts

Cross-platform development isn't just a trend—it's the **future of software engineering.** With tools like **Python, C#, and .NET Core**, developers can build **scalable, secure, and high-performance applications** that run anywhere.

In the next chapter, we'll explore **how to choose the right tech stack** for your cross-platform project.

Key   Takeaways
Cross-platform coding allows you to write once and run anywhere, saving development time and costs.
Python offers simplicity and flexibility, C# delivers high performance, and .NET Core ensures seamless multi-platform   support.
Common myths about cross-platform development are outdated—modern tools make it **fast, efficient, and scalable.**

CHAPTER 2

CHOOSING THE RIGHT TECH STACK

Developing cross-platform applications requires selecting the right technologies based on **performance, scalability, maintainability, and development speed**. Python, C#, and .NET Core each have their own strengths and ideal use cases. Choosing the best tech stack depends on your project's needs.

When to Use Python vs. C# vs. .NET Core

Each language and framework has its own unique advantages and trade-offs. Let's explore when to use **Python, C#, and .NET Core** for cross-platform development.

Technology Best Used For

Python	Web applications, scripting, AI/ML, automation, APIs, and cross-platform desktop tools
C#	High-performance applications, enterprise software, game development, and Windows-focused apps
.NET Core	Scalable web apps, cross-platform enterprise applications, cloud-based services, and microservices

When to Use Python

Rapid Development: Python's simple syntax makes it perfect for fast prototyping.
Cross-Platform Support: Runs smoothly on **Windows, macOS, and Linux** without modifications.
AI & Machine Learning: Python dominates in **data science, AI, and automation** (TensorFlow, PyTorch).
Web & API Development: With **FastAPI, Flask, Django**, Python is widely used for backend services.
Automation & Scripting: Great for automating repetitive tasks and working with system processes.

29

Not Ideal for:

- Low-latency applications (e.g., game engines, real-time systems).
- Heavy computational tasks (C++ or C# performs better).

When to Use C#

Performance & Speed: C# is **faster** than Python due to **compiled execution** and memory management. **Game Development:** Unity (one of the most popular game engines) is built on C#. **Enterprise & Desktop Applications:** .NET-powered C# is a standard in **banking, healthcare, and finance**. **Windows Development:** Seamless integration with Windows APIs, including **WPF and UWP**.

Not Ideal for:

- AI & ML (Python has better libraries).
- Scripting and quick automation tasks.

When to Use .NET Core

Truly Cross-Platform: Unlike the original .NET Framework, .NET Core runs **natively on Windows, Linux, and   macOS**.

Web & API Development: ASP.NET Core is an excellent choice for **scalable** **web** **services**. **Cloud & Microservices:** Microsoft's Azure heavily supports .NET Core. **Enterprise-Grade Security:** Trusted by large organizations for **secure web and business applications**.

Not Ideal for:

- AI/ML (Python is more optimized).
- Rapid prototyping (Python is quicker).

Strengths and Weaknesses of Each Language

Feature	Python	C#	.NET Core
Ease of Learning	Easy	Moderate	Moderate
Performance	Slower	High	High
Scalability	Good	Excellent	Excellent
Web Development	Strong (Django, Flask)	Strong (ASP.NET)	Strong (ASP.NET Core)

31

Feature	Python	C#	.NET Core
AI & ML	Best Choice	Limited	Limited
Game Development	Limited	Best Choice (Unity)	Limited
Enterprise Use	Common	Standard	Strong
Cloud & Microservices	Good	Good	Best Choice
Cross-Platform Compatibility	Native	Windows Focused (before .NET Core)	Best Choice
Security	Good	Excellent	Enterprise-Grade

Each language has specific areas where it shines. If **AI & automation** are key, **Python** is the best choice. If performance and enterprise software are priorities, **C# & .NET Core** are ideal.

Industry Use Cases

Here are real-world examples of where each language and framework is most commonly used:

Python in Action

Google & AI: Python powers **Google's AI & deep learning frameworks** (TensorFlow). **Instagram:** The backend runs on Django (Python). **Netflix:** Uses Python for content recommendations. **Spotify:** Python helps in backend services and music data analysis.

Example Use Case: A startup building an AI-powered chatbot would likely choose **Python** due to its rich AI/ML libraries.

C# in Action

Microsoft Products: Office, Teams, and Windows applications. **Unity Games:** Popular games like **Pokemon Go** use C# in Unity. **Enterprise Software:** Many financial firms use C# for **high-performance trading platforms**.

33

Example Use Case: A gaming studio developing a **high-performance 3D game** would pick **C# with Unity**.

.NET Core in Action

Stack Overflow: The world's largest developer Q&A platform runs on .NET Core.
Azure Cloud Services: Microsoft's cloud services heavily integrate .NET Core.
Finance & Banking: Large firms use .NET Core for **secure web APIs & backend processing**.

Example Use Case: A **global bank** needing a **secure, scalable web application** would choose **.NET Core with C#**.

Conclusion: How to Choose the Right Stack?

Ask Yourself These Questions:
What is the project's primary goal?

- AI/ML, automation → **Python**
- Enterprise software, games → **C#**
- Scalable, secure web apps → **.NET Core**

Does performance matter?

- Need fast execution? → **C# or .NET Core**
- Need flexibility? → **Python**

Who will be using the application?

- **Windows-based audience?** → C# or .NET Core
- **Cross-platform web app?** → Python or .NET Core

How much time do you have?

- **Need fast development?** → Python
- **Need robust security?** → .NET Core

What is the future of the application?

- **Scaling up?** → .NET Core
- **AI-powered?** → Python

By understanding the strengths and weaknesses of **Python, C#, and .NET Core**, developers can **make informed decisions** that lead to successful, scalable, and future-proof applications.

Key   Takeaways

Python is best for AI, automation, and quick development.

C# is ideal for high-performance applications, enterprise software, and game development.
.NET Core is the best choice for scalable, secure, and cloud-based   web   applications.
Choosing the right tech stack depends on project goals, performance needs, and industry demands.

Next Chapter: Setting Up Your Development Environment for Cross-Platform Coding

CHAPTER 3

SETTING UP YOUR DEVELOPMENT ENVIRONMENT

A well-configured development environment is essential for **efficient** and **error-free** cross-platform development. This chapter covers **installing the necessary tools**, **configuring workflows**, and **using version control effectively**.

Installing Necessary Tools

Choosing the Right Code Editor/IDE

Different projects require different tools. Below are the most commonly used options:

Editor/IDE	Best For	Platforms
Visual Studio Code (VS Code)	Python & C# development, lightweight, extensible	Windows, macOS, Linux

Editor/IDE	Best For	Platforms
Visual Studio (VS)	Full-fledged .NET & C# development	Windows, macOS
PyCharm	Python development	Windows, macOS, Linux
JetBrains Rider	.NET Core & C#	Windows, macOS, Linux

For most **cross-platform projects**, **VS Code** is the best choice due to its **lightweight nature and extensive plugin ecosystem**.

Installing Python

Python needs to be installed on your system to run scripts and backend applications.

Installation Steps

1. **Download the latest version** from Python's official site.
2. **Check "Add Python to PATH"** during installation to make it accessible from the command line.
3. Verify installation:

```sh

python --version
```

4. Install package manager `pip`:

```sh


python -m ensurepip --default-pip
```

Recommended Python Packages for Cross-Platform Development

Install commonly used Python libraries:

```sh


pip install flask fastapi numpy pandas requests
```

Installing .NET SDK

.NET SDK is required to build C# applications.

Installation Steps

1. Download **.NET SDK** from Microsoft's official site.
2. Install using the default settings.
3. Verify installation:

```sh

```

```
dotnet --version
```

4. Create a test .NET project:

```sh
dotnet new console -o TestApp
cd TestApp
dotnet run
```

Installing Git for Version Control

Git helps track changes and collaborate efficiently.

Installation Steps

1. Download and install **Git** from git-scm.com.
2. Verify installation:

```sh
git --version
```

3. Set up user details:

```sh
git config --global user.name "Your Name"
git config --global user.email "your.email@example.com"
```

40

4. Initialize a new Git repository:

```sh

git init
```

Configuring Cross-Platform Workflows

A good workflow ensures smooth development across **Windows, macOS, and Linux**.

Using Virtual Environments in Python

Virtual environments prevent conflicts between dependencies.

Setup a Virtual Environment
```sh

python -m venv myenv
source myenv/bin/activate   # On macOS/Linux
myenv\Scripts\activate   # On Windows
```

To deactivate:

```sh

deactivate
```

Managing Dependencies in .NET Core

.NET Core uses `NuGet` for package management.

Install a Package

sh

```
dotnet add package Newtonsoft.Json
```

Running Python & C# Code in VS Code

1. **Install VS Code extensions:**
   - o Python extension
   - o C# extension
   - o Docker (for containerization)
2. **Configure `launch.json` for Debugging:**
   - o Open `.vscode/launch.json`
   - o Add configurations for Python & C#
3. **Run Python Code:**

   sh

   ```
   python main.py
   ```

4. **Run .NET Code:**

   sh

42

```
dotnet run
```

Version Control Best Practices (Git & GitHub)

GitHub is a must for managing cross-platform projects effectively.

Setting Up a GitHub Repository

1. **Create a repository** on GitHub.
2. **Clone the repository:**

   sh

   ```
   git                              clone
   https://github.com/yourusername/repositor
   y.git
   ```

3. **Add & Commit Changes:**

   sh

   ```
   git add .
   git commit -m "Initial commit"
   ```

4. **Push Changes to GitHub:**

   sh

```
git push origin main
```

Git Branching Strategy

Use **branches** to manage different features or versions.

```sh
sh

git checkout -b feature-branch   # Create a new
branch
git checkout main   # Switch back to the main
branch
git merge feature-branch   # Merge changes
```

Automating Workflows with GitHub Actions

GitHub Actions allows automatic testing & deployment.

1. **Create a `.github/workflows/ci.yml` file**
2. **Example GitHub Action for Python & .NET CI/CD:**

```yaml
yaml

name: CI/CD Pipeline

on:
  push:
    branches:
      - main
```

```
jobs:
  build:
    runs-on: ubuntu-latest
    steps:
      - uses: actions/checkout@v3
      - name: Set up Python
        uses: actions/setup-python@v3
        with:
          python-version: '3.9'
      - name: Install dependencies
        run: pip install -r requirements.txt
      - name: Run tests
        run: pytest

      - name: Set up .NET
        uses: actions/setup-dotnet@v3
        with:
          dotnet-version: '7.0'
      - name: Build .NET project
        run:   dotnet   build   --configuration
Release
```

Conclusion: Ensuring a Productive Development Setup

Key Takeaways

VS Code, Visual Studio, or PyCharm are excellent for cross-platform coding.

Python & .NET SDK installations are necessary for development.

Virtual environments & NuGet help manage dependencies efficiently.

Git & GitHub ensure smooth collaboration and version tracking.

GitHub Actions automates testing & deployment.

Next Chapter: Understanding .NET Core for Multi-Platform Applications

CHAPTER 4

UNDERSTANDING .NET CORE FOR MULTI-PLATFORM APPLICATIONS

.NET Core has revolutionized cross-platform development by allowing **C# applications** to run on **Windows, macOS, and Linux** seamlessly. This chapter covers why .NET Core is the **future of C#**, how to run .NET applications on different operating systems, and whether to use the **.NET CLI** or **Visual Studio** for development.

Why .NET Core is the Future of C#

.NET Core is an **open-source, cross-platform** framework developed by Microsoft, designed to replace the older **.NET Framework**, which was Windows-exclusive.

The Evolution of .NET

Before .NET Core, C# developers used the **.NET Framework**, which had limitations:

47

Great   for   Windows   development

Couldn't   run   natively   on   Linux/macOS

Large and monolithic

Microsoft introduced **.NET Core** to solve these issues. With **.NET Core**, developers can: Build truly **cross-platform** applications Develop **lightweight, high-performance** applications Use **open-source tools and frameworks** Deploy applications on **cloud services like Azure, AWS, and Google Cloud**

.NET Core vs. .NET Framework

Feature	.NET Core	.NET Framework
Cross-Platform	Yes (Windows, Linux, macOS)	Windows only
Performance	Faster (optimized runtime)	Slower
Microservices Support	Best choice	Limited

Feature	.NET Core	.NET Framework
Open Source	Fully open-source	Proprietary
Future Development	Actively developed	No longer updated

Why Developers Are Moving to .NET Core

- **Performance Boost**: Faster execution than the .NET Framework.
- **Docker & Cloud-Ready**: Works seamlessly with **containers and Kubernetes**.
- **Better Dependency Management**: No need for system-wide .NET installation.
- **Unified Platform**: Supports **desktop, web, mobile, IoT, and AI** development.

With **.NET 5, .NET 6, and .NET 7**, Microsoft has **merged .NET Core and .NET Framework** into a single platform called **.NET (modern version)**.

Running .NET Applications on Windows, Linux, and macOS

.NET Core allows you to **write once, run anywhere**, making it perfect for **cross-platform deployment**.

Installing .NET Core on Different Operating Systems

Windows

1. Download and install .NET SDK from Microsoft's .NET download page.
2. Verify installation:

```sh
dotnet --version
```

macOS

1. Install **Homebrew** (if not installed):

```sh
/bin/bash -c "$(curl -fsSL https://raw.githubusercontent.com/Homebrew/install/HEAD/install.sh)"
```

50

2. Install .NET Core:

```sh

brew install --cask dotnet-sdk
```

3. Verify installation:

```sh

dotnet --version
```

Linux (Ubuntu/Debian)

1. Install dependencies:

```sh

sudo apt update && sudo apt install -y dotnet-sdk-7.0
```

2. Verify installation:

```sh

dotnet --version
```

51

Creating and Running a .NET Core Application

Once .NET Core is installed, let's create a **simple console application**.

Step 1: Create a New .NET Core Project

Run the following command to create a new console app:

```sh
```

```sh
dotnet new console -o MyFirstApp
cd MyFirstApp
```

Step 2: Modify the Code

Open `Program.cs` and modify the code:

```csharp
```

```csharp
using System;

class Program
{
    static void Main()
    {
        Console.WriteLine("Hello, Cross-Platform World!");
    }
```

```
}
```

Step 3: Run the Application

```sh
sh
```

```
dotnet run
```

The output should be:

```sql
sql
```

```
Hello, Cross-Platform World!
```

Step 4: Publish for Different Platforms

To package the application for different OS:

- **For Windows:**

  ```sh
  sh
  ```

  ```
  dotnet publish -c Release -r win-x64 --
  self-contained true
  ```

- **For Linux:**

  ```sh
  sh
  ```

```
dotnet publish -c Release -r linux-x64 --
self-contained true
```

- **For macOS:**

```sh
sh
```

```
dotnet publish -c Release -r osx-x64 --
self-contained true
```

This generates a **standalone executable** that can run on the target system **without requiring .NET Core to be installed**.

.NET CLI vs. Visual Studio: Which One to Use?

.NET CLI (Command-Line Interface)

.NET CLI is a **lightweight, command-line-based tool** for .NET Core development.

When to Use .NET CLI?

For quick prototyping and scripting

For automation in CI/CD pipelines

For headless development on Linux/macOS

When working with Docker & cloud-native development

Common .NET CLI Commands

Command	Description
`dotnet new console -o AppName`	Create a new console app
`dotnet run`	Run the application
`dotnet build`	Compile the application
`dotnet publish`	Package for deployment
`dotnet add package <package-name>`	Add a NuGet package

Visual Studio & Visual Studio Code

Visual Studio (Windows/macOS) and **VS Code (cross-platform)** provide **graphical tools** for .NET Core development.

When to Use Visual Studio?

For large-scale enterprise applications

When debugging complex C# applications

For WPF, .NET MAUI, or Blazor development

When to Use VS Code?

For lightweight development

For Python + .NET Core projects

For working on Linux/macOS

Choosing Between .NET CLI and Visual Studio

Feature	.NET CLI	Visual Studio
Installation Size	Small	Large
Ease of Use	Requires CLI knowledge	User-friendly
Debugging Tools	Minimal	Advanced
CI/CD Automation	Great for DevOps	Not CLI-friendly
Cross-Platform	Yes	Only VS Code

Best Approach:

- Use **.NET CLI** for quick builds, scripting, and cloud-based workflows.
- Use **Visual Studio** for enterprise applications and heavy debugging.

Conclusion: The Power of .NET Core for Cross-Platform Development

Key Takeaways

.NET Core is the future of C# development, replacing the Windows-only .NET Framework. It runs **natively** on **Windows, macOS, and Linux**, making it ideal for cross-platform applications. **.NET CLI** is lightweight and powerful for DevOps, while **Visual Studio** offers a full-fledged development experience. **Publishing .NET apps for multiple platforms** is easy with `dotnet publish`.

Next Chapter: Python's Role in Cross-Platform Solutions

CHAPTER 5

PYTHON'S ROLE IN CROSS-PLATFORM SOLUTIONS

Python has become a **cornerstone of modern development**, thanks to its simplicity, versatility, and ability to run seamlessly on **Windows, Linux, and macOS**. When combined with **.NET Core**, Python enhances **backend functionality, automation, AI/ML capabilities, and scripting** in cross-platform applications.

How Python Complements .NET Core

.NET Core is optimized for **high-performance, enterprise-grade applications**, while Python excels at **automation, data science, AI, and rapid prototyping**. Together, they provide a **powerful combination** for building **scalable, flexible, and cross-platform applications**.

Why Use Python Alongside .NET Core?

Rapid Development – Python allows quick prototyping, while .NET Core provides production-level performance.

Data Processing & AI – Python's **NumPy, Pandas, and TensorFlow** enhance .NET applications with **data analysis & AI**.

Automation & Scripting – Python is excellent for **task automation** in .NET Core applications.

Microservices & APIs – Python's **FastAPI and Flask** can handle **API services**, while .NET Core powers the main application.

Cross-Platform Interoperability – Python scripts can be executed **within .NET applications** using **Python.NET and IronPython**.

How Python and .NET Core Work Together

Use Case	Python's Role	.NET Core's Role
Data Analysis & AI	TensorFlow, Pandas, SciPy	Frontend & UI
Automation	Automates file handling, cloud tasks	Runs the main business logic

Use Case	Python's Role	.NET Core's Role
APIs & Web Services	FastAPI, Flask for microservices	ASP.NET Core for main APIs
Game Development	AI-based bots & logic in Python	Unity (C#) for graphics & physics

Python is often used **alongside .NET Core**, rather than as a replacement, making cross-platform development **faster and more efficient**.

Using Python for Backend, Scripting, and Automation

Python is **lightweight and flexible**, making it an excellent choice for backend services, automation scripts, and system-level programming.

Python as a Backend in Cross-Platform Applications

Python is widely used in **web development, API services, and microservices**. Popular frameworks include:

- **Flask** – Lightweight framework for small applications.

- **Django** – Full-stack web framework for enterprise apps.
- **FastAPI** – High-performance API framework for microservices.

Example: Creating a REST API in Python (FastAPI)

```python

from fastapi import FastAPI

app = FastAPI()

@app.get("/")
def read_root():
    return {"message": "Hello from Python API"}

# Run the API
# uvicorn filename:app --reload
```

This **FastAPI-powered Python backend** can integrate with a **.NET Core frontend** using **HTTP requests**.

Python for Scripting & Automation

Python can automate **system tasks, file operations, database management, and cloud functions**.

Example: Automating File Handling in Python

```python
import os

# List files in a directory
files = os.listdir("C:/Users/")

# Move files based on extension
for file in files:
    if file.endswith(".txt"):
        os.rename(file, "C:/Backup/" + file)

print("File transfer completed.")
```

Use Cases

- Automating **database backups** for .NET applications.
- Running **scheduled tasks** on cloud platforms (AWS Lambda, Azure Functions).
- Integrating with **PowerShell** or **Bash scripts** for DevOps.

Example: Running a Python Script in a .NET Core Application

Use Python inside a **C# application** to execute automation tasks:

```csharp
using System;
using System.Diagnostics;

class Program
{
    static void Main()
    {
        Process process = new Process();
        process.StartInfo.FileName = "python";
        process.StartInfo.Arguments        =
"script.py"; // Python script to run

process.StartInfo.RedirectStandardOutput = true;
        process.StartInfo.UseShellExecute        =
false;
        process.Start();
        string                output        =
process.StandardOutput.ReadToEnd();
        Console.WriteLine(output);
    }
}
```

Key Python Libraries for Cross-Platform Development

Python's **power lies in its libraries**, which support everything from **automation to machine learning**.

Best Python Libraries for .NET & Cross-Platform Apps

Category	Library	Use Case
Web APIs	Flask, FastAPI, Django	Backend development
Data Processing	Pandas, NumPy	Data analysis, finance apps
AI & ML	TensorFlow, Scikit-learn	AI-powered apps
Automation	PyAutoGUI, Selenium	UI automation
Database Handling	SQLAlchemy, Psycopg2	SQL & NoSQL databases
System Integration	PyWin32, subprocess	Running OS-level commands
.NET Interoperability	Python.NET, IronPython	Running Python in .NET

Integrating Python with .NET Core

Microsoft provides **Python.NET** and **IronPython**, allowing Python and .NET Core applications to work together.

Example: Calling Python from C# using Python.NET

```csharp
using Python.Runtime;

class Program
{
    static void Main()
    {
        using (Py.GIL()) // Initialize Python environment
        {
            dynamic py = Py.Import("math");
            Console.WriteLine(py.sqrt(16));   // Calls Python's math.sqrt()
        }
    }
}
```

Conclusion: Why Python is a Key Player in Cross-Platform Development

Key Takeaways

Python enhances .NET Core applications by providing automation, scripting, and AI capabilities. **Using Python for backend services**, APIs, and microservices speeds up development. **Python.NET & IronPython** enable seamless integration between Python and C#. **Python's cross-platform libraries** support web, data, AI, and system automation.

Next Chapter: Cross-Platform UI Development: WPF, MAUI, and Blazor

PART 2

CROSS-PLATFORM ARCHITECTURE & FRAMEWORKS

CHAPTER 6

CROSS-PLATFORM UI DEVELOPMENT: WPF, MAUI, AND BLAZOR

Developing user interfaces that run seamlessly across **Windows, macOS, Linux, Android, and iOS** requires powerful **cross-platform UI frameworks**. In the .NET ecosystem, the top choices for cross-platform UI development are:

.NET MAUI (Multi-platform App UI) – For **native mobile & desktop apps**

Blazor – For **interactive web apps with C# & .NET Core**

WPF (Windows Presentation Foundation) – For **Windows-only desktop applications**

This chapter covers how to use **.NET MAUI and Blazor** to create **cross-platform UIs** efficiently.

.NET MAUI: The Evolution of Xamarin

What is .NET MAUI?

.NET MAUI (Multi-platform App UI) is Microsoft's **next-generation** framework for building **native** applications across:

- **Windows**
- **macOS**
- **iOS**
- **Android**

.NET MAUI **replaces Xamarin**, providing a **single project structure** to develop applications for multiple platforms.

Why Use .NET MAUI?

Single Codebase – Write **one C# & XAML UI** for multiple platforms.

Native Performance – Apps run with **native UI components** for each platform.

Deep Integration with .NET – Uses **.NET 7+** and **C#**, reducing dependency issues.

Hot Reload Support – Developers can see changes **instantly** without restarting the app.

69

Setting Up a .NET MAUI Project

Step 1: Install .NET MAUI

Install the **.NET SDK** from Microsoft's official site. Install MAUI using the command:

sh

```
dotnet workload install maui
```

Create a new MAUI project:

sh

```
dotnet new maui -n MyFirstMauiApp
cd MyFirstMauiApp
```

Step 2: Run Your App on Different Platforms

- Run on **Windows**:

  sh

  ```
  dotnet build -t:Run -f net7.0-windows10.0.19041.0
  ```

- Run on **macOS**:

  sh

70

```
dotnet build -t:Run -f net7.0-macos
```

- Run on **Android**:

```sh
sh
```

```
dotnet build -t:Run -f net7.0-android
```

- Run on **iOS** (Mac required):

```sh
sh
```

```
dotnet build -t:Run -f net7.0-ios
```

Step 3: Modify the UI

Open `MainPage.xaml` and modify the UI:

```xml
xml
```

```xml
<ContentPage
xmlns="http://schemas.microsoft.com/dotnet/2021/maui"

xmlns:x="http://schemas.microsoft.com/winfx/2009/xaml"
            x:Class="MyFirstMauiApp.MainPage">
   <VerticalStackLayout>
      <Label Text="Welcome to .NET MAUI!"
             FontSize="24"
```

```
                    HorizontalOptions="Center"/>
        <Button        Text="Click        Me"
Clicked="OnButtonClick"/>
    </VerticalStackLayout>
</ContentPage>
```

Modify the C# event handler in `MainPage.xaml.cs`:

```csharp

private   void   OnButtonClick(object   sender,
EventArgs e)
{
    DisplayAlert("Message",   "Hello   from   .NET
MAUI!", "OK");
}
```

This will create a native UI app that runs on Windows, macOS, Android, and iOS!

Blazor: Building Interactive Web UIs

What is Blazor?

Blazor is a **C#-based web framework** that allows developers to build **interactive UIs** for web applications using **C# instead of JavaScript**.

Blazor   provides:

Blazor WebAssembly – Runs Blazor apps **directly in the browser** (like JavaScript).

Blazor Server – Runs on the **server**, sending UI updates to the client.

Blazor Hybrid – Integrates with **.NET MAUI** for cross-platform desktop & mobile apps.

Why Use Blazor?

Full-stack C# development – No need for JavaScript.

Reusability – Blazor components can be used across web & mobile.

Native Performance – WebAssembly allows near-native speed in browsers.

Integrated with .NET – Works with **ASP.NET Core, Entity Framework, and .NET APIs**.

Building a Blazor WebAssembly App

Step 1: Create a New Blazor Project

Run the following command to create a Blazor WebAssembly project:

```sh
```

```sh
dotnet new blazorwasm -o MyBlazorApp
cd MyBlazorApp
```

Step 2: Run the Application

```sh
```

```sh
dotnet run
```

Open `https://localhost:5001` in your browser – the Blazor UI will load!

Comparing .NET MAUI vs. Blazor

Feature	.NET MAUI	Blazor
Best For	Mobile & desktop apps	Web applications
Platforms	Windows, macOS, Android, iOS	Browsers (WebAssembly)
Uses XAML?	Yes	No
Uses C# for UI?	Yes	Yes

Feature	.NET MAUI	Blazor
Replaces JavaScript?	No	Yes
Supports Offline Mode?	Yes	Yes (Blazor WebAssembly)

Conclusion: Choosing the Right UI Framework for Cross-Platform Development

Key Takeaways

.NET MAUI is perfect for **native mobile & desktop apps** using a **single codebase**. **Blazor** enables developers to build **interactive web UIs** using C# instead of JavaScript. **.NET MAUI + Blazor Hybrid** is a powerful combination for **building full-stack cross-platform applications**.

Next Chapter: Building APIs That Work Across Platforms (REST vs. GraphQL, FastAPI vs. ASP.NET Core Web API)

CHAPTER 7

BUILDING APIS THAT WORK ACROSS PLATFORMS

APIs (Application Programming Interfaces) act as **bridges** between different applications, allowing them to communicate across platforms. Choosing the **right API architecture** is essential for **scalability, performance, and maintainability**. This chapter covers:

REST vs. GraphQL: When to Use Each
FastAPI (Python) vs. ASP.NET Core Web API: A Performance   Comparison
How to Structure API Endpoints for Scalability

REST vs. GraphQL: Which One to Use?

Two of the most widely used API architectures are **REST (Representational State Transfer)** and **GraphQL**.

What is REST?

RESTful APIs follow **standard HTTP methods** (GET, POST, PUT, DELETE) and return **JSON responses**. **Simple & widely adopted**
Follows CRUD principles (Create, Read, Update, Delete)
Easy to cache and scale

What is GraphQL?

GraphQL is a **query language** that allows clients to request only the data they need. **Flexible, client-defined queries**
Reduces over-fetching & under-fetching
More efficient for complex data retrieval

Key Differences: REST vs. GraphQL

Feature	REST API	GraphQL API
Data Fetching	Fixed endpoints	Dynamic queries
Performance	Can over-fetch data	Efficient, only fetches what's needed
Request Complexity	Multiple requests needed for related data	Single request for multiple data points

Feature	REST API	GraphQL API
Best For	Simple operations	CRUD Complex relationships between data

When to Use REST vs. GraphQL

Use **REST** when **simplicity, caching, and statelessness** are important.

Use **GraphQL** when **reducing over-fetching** and optimizing queries for mobile clients.

FastAPI (Python) vs. ASP.NET Core Web API

Both **FastAPI (Python)** and **ASP.NET Core Web API** are excellent choices for **building scalable, high-performance APIs**.

Why Use FastAPI?

Blazing fast (built on Starlette & Pydantic)
Auto-generates OpenAPI & Swagger docs
Asynchronous support (async/await)
Best for AI, ML, and data-driven applications

Why Use ASP.NET Core Web API?

Enterprise-grade API framework

Deep integration with .NET ecosystem

High-performance, multithreaded support

Best for large-scale business applications

Performance Comparison

Feature	FastAPI (Python)	ASP.NET Core Web API
Speed	Fast (async support)	Faster (compiled code)
Ease of Development	Simple & lightweight	Great for large projects
Scalability	High	Very High
Auto-generated Docs	Yes (Swagger, OpenAPI)	Yes (Swagger, OpenAPI)

Building a REST API: FastAPI vs. ASP.NET Core Web API

Creating a Simple API in FastAPI (Python)

Install FastAPI & Uvicorn:

```sh
pip install fastapi uvicorn
```

Create main.py:

```python
from fastapi import FastAPI

app = FastAPI()

@app.get("/")
def read_root():
    return {"message": "Hello from FastAPI"}

@app.get("/users/{user_id}")
def read_user(user_id: int):
    return {"user_id": user_id}
```

Run the API:

```sh
uvicorn main:app --reload
```

Access Swagger Docs at:

```bash
http://localhost:8000/docs
```

Creating a Simple API in ASP.NET Core Web API (C#)

Create a new ASP.NET Core API project:

```sh
dotnet new webapi -n MyApi
cd MyApi
```

Modify Controllers/WeatherForecastController.cs:

```csharp
using Microsoft.AspNetCore.Mvc;

[ApiController]
[Route("[controller]")]
public class UserController : ControllerBase
{
    [HttpGet("{id}")]
    public IActionResult GetUser(int id)
    {
```

81

```
        return Ok(new { user_id = id, name =
"John Doe" });
    }
}
```

Run the API:

```
sh
```

```
dotnet run
```

Access Swagger Docs at:

```
bash
```

```
http://localhost:5000/swagger
```

Structuring API Endpoints for Scalability

A well-structured API ensures **maintainability, security, and high performance**.

Best Practices for Designing Scalable APIs

Use Versioning – `/v1/users/` instead of `/users/`
Follow RESTful Naming Conventions – GET `/users`,
POST `/users`, DELETE `/users/{id}`
Optimize Query Performance – Use **pagination, caching,**

and **indexing**

Secure APIs with Authentication – Use **JWT, OAuth, or API keys**

Example: Structuring an API with Best Practices

Endpoint	HTTP Method	Purpose
/api/v1/users	GET	Get all users
/api/v1/users/{id}	GET	Get a single user by ID
/api/v1/users	POST	Create a new user
/api/v1/users/{id}	PUT	Update user information
/api/v1/users/{id}	DELETE	Remove a user

Example JSON Response for GET /users/1

```json

{
    "id": 1,
```

```
"name": "John Doe",
"email": "john@example.com"
}
```

Conclusion: Choosing the Right API for Cross-Platform Development

Key Takeaways

REST is simple and widely used, while **GraphQL** is flexible for complex data queries. **FastAPI** is ideal for **AI, ML, and rapid development**, while **ASP.NET Core** is best for **high-performance enterprise applications**. **Scalable API design** includes **versioning, security, and performance optimization**.

Next Chapter: Database Management in a Multi-Platform World (SQL vs. NoSQL, Entity Framework, Django ORM)

CHAPTER 8

DATABASE MANAGEMENT IN A MULTI-PLATFORM WORLD

Databases are the **backbone** of modern applications, and choosing the right one is critical for **performance, scalability, and maintainability**. In this chapter, we will explore:

SQL vs. NoSQL: Choosing the Right Database
Working with PostgreSQL, MongoDB, and SQL Server
Using Entity Framework Core and Django ORM

SQL vs. NoSQL: Choosing the Right Database

Before selecting a database, it's important to understand the differences between **SQL (relational) databases** and **NoSQL (non-relational) databases**.

What is SQL?

SQL (Structured Query Language) databases use a **fixed schema** with **tables, rows, and relationships**.

Best for **structured data**
Strong **ACID compliance** (Atomicity, Consistency, Isolation, Durability)
Supports **complex queries and transactions**

Examples:

- PostgreSQL
- MySQL
- Microsoft SQL Server
- SQLite

What is NoSQL?

NoSQL databases store data in **key-value, document, column-family, or graph formats**. They are **schema-less**, meaning they can store flexible and unstructured data.

Best for **big data and real-time applications**
Highly **scalable and distributed**
Supports **JSON-like document storage**

Examples:

- MongoDB (Document-based)
- Redis (Key-value store)
- Cassandra (Column-family store)

Choosing Between SQL and NoSQL

Feature	SQL Databases	NoSQL Databases
Data Structure	Structured (tables)	Unstructured (JSON, key-value)
Best For	Transactions & complex queries	High scalability & big data
Schema	Fixed schema	Dynamic schema
Scalability	Vertical (scale-up)	Horizontal (scale-out)
Consistency	Strong (ACID)	Eventual consistency
Examples	PostgreSQL, SQL Server	MongoDB, Redis, Cassandra

When to Use SQL vs. NoSQL

Use SQL for **finance, banking, e-commerce, and applications needing strong data integrity**.

87

Use NoSQL for **social media, big data analytics, IoT, and flexible document storage**.

Working with PostgreSQL, MongoDB, and SQL Server

PostgreSQL: The Best Open-Source SQL Database

PostgreSQL is a **high-performance, open-source relational database** known for: **ACID compliance JSONB support** (Hybrid SQL + NoSQL capabilities) **Extensibility & scalability**

Installing PostgreSQL

Windows/Linux/macOS:

- Download from PostgreSQL official site
- Verify installation:

```sh
psql --version
```

Creating a Database and Table

```sql
sql


CREATE DATABASE myapp;
\c myapp

CREATE TABLE users (
    id SERIAL PRIMARY KEY,
    name VARCHAR(50),
    email VARCHAR(100) UNIQUE
);
```

Insert Data & Query

```sql
sql


INSERT INTO users (name, email) VALUES ('John
Doe', 'john@example.com');

SELECT * FROM users;
```

MongoDB: The Leading NoSQL Database

MongoDB is a **document-oriented NoSQL database** that stores data in **JSON-like BSON format**.

Best for **big data, analytics, and flexible schemas** Supports **horizontal scaling** **High availability** with built-in replication

89

Installing MongoDB

Windows/Linux/macOS:

- Download from MongoDB official site
- Start MongoDB service:

```sh
```

```
mongod --dbpath /data/db
```

Creating a Database and Collection

```sh
```

```
mongo
use myapp
db.users.insertOne({ "name": "Alice", "email": "alice@example.com" })
db.users.find()
```

Microsoft SQL Server: The Enterprise Solution

Microsoft SQL Server is a **powerful, enterprise-grade relational database** designed for **high availability and performance**.

Best for **corporate applications, BI, and analytics**
Integration with .NET and Azure
Strong security features

Installing SQL Server

Windows:

- Download from Microsoft SQL Server
- Use **SQL Server Management Studio (SSMS)** for GUI
  management.

Creating a Database and Table

sql

```sql
CREATE DATABASE MyApp;
USE MyApp;

CREATE TABLE Users (
    ID INT PRIMARY KEY IDENTITY(1,1),
    Name NVARCHAR(50),
    Email NVARCHAR(100) UNIQUE
);
```

Using Entity Framework Core and Django ORM

What is Entity Framework Core (EF Core)?

Entity Framework Core (EF Core) is **Microsoft's ORM (Object-Relational Mapper)** that simplifies database interactions in **.NET applications**.

Supports **PostgreSQL, SQL Server, MySQL, and SQLite** Allows **LINQ-based queries** instead of raw SQL Automatically **generates database schemas**

Setting Up EF Core in .NET

Install EF Core for PostgreSQL:

```sh
dotnet                    add                    package
Npgsql.EntityFrameworkCore.PostgreSQL
```

Define a **C# Model**:

```csharp
public class User
{
    public int Id { get; set; }
    public string Name { get; set; }
    public string Email { get; set; }
}
```

Configure **DbContext**:

```csharp
public class AppDbContext : DbContext
{
    public DbSet<User> Users { get; set; }

    protected          override          void
OnConfiguring(DbContextOptionsBuilder options)
        =>
options.UseNpgsql("Host=localhost;Database=myap
p;Username=postgres;Password=mypassword");
}
```

Apply **Migrations & Update Database**:

```sh
dotnet ef migrations add InitialCreate
dotnet ef database update
```

What is Django ORM?

Django ORM (Object-Relational Mapper) simplifies database handling in **Python applications**.

Automatically **creates and updates database schemas** Works with **PostgreSQL, MySQL, and SQLite** Uses **Python models instead of SQL queries**

93

Setting Up Django ORM

Install Django & PostgreSQL adapter:

sh

```
pip install django psycopg2
```

Define a **Django Model** (models.py):

python

```
from django.db import models

class User(models.Model):
    name = models.CharField(max_length=50)
    email = models.EmailField(unique=True)
```

Apply **Migrations & Update Database**:

sh

```
python manage.py makemigrations
python manage.py migrate
```

Conclusion: Choosing the Right Database for Your
Project

Key Takeaways

SQL databases (PostgreSQL, SQL Server) are best for
structured data and transactions.
NoSQL databases (MongoDB) are best for **big data and
real-time applications**.
Entity Framework Core makes database interactions
easier in **.NET applications**.
Django ORM simplifies database management in **Python
applications**.

**Next Chapter: Microservices Architecture with Python
& .NET Core**

CHAPTER 9

MICROSERVICES ARCHITECTURE WITH PYTHON & .NET CORE

Microservices architecture has transformed how modern applications are built, making them **scalable, maintainable, and independent**. In this chapter, we will explore:

What are microservices?
Implementing microservices using FastAPI (Python) & .NET Core
Containerizing microservices with Docker

What Are Microservices?

Microservices architecture is a **modular approach** to application development, where an application is broken down into **small, independent services** that communicate via **APIs**.

Key Characteristics of Microservices

Independent Deployment – Each service can be deployed separately.

Scalability – Services can scale individually based on demand.

Technology Agnostic – Different services can be written in **Python, .NET, or any language**.

Resilience & Fault Isolation – A failure in one service does not crash the entire system.

DevOps & CI/CD Friendly – Microservices are **easier to automate and update**.

Microservices vs. Monolithic Architecture

Feature	Monolithic Architecture	Microservices Architecture
Scalability	Hard to scale	Easily scalable
Deployment	Entire app must be redeployed	Independent deployment per service
Technology Choice	Limited to one stack	Multiple languages & frameworks
Fault Tolerance	A failure can crash the entire app	Services fail independently

Feature	Monolithic Architecture	Microservices Architecture
Best For	Small apps	Large, complex applications

When to Use Microservices?

Large applications with high scalability needs
Systems requiring modular development (e.g., e-commerce, fintech, SaaS)
Applications with frequent updates and CI/CD integration

Implementing Microservices Using FastAPI & .NET Core

Microservices can be built using **Python (FastAPI)** and **C# (.NET Core Web API)**, working together as **independent services**.

Microservice 1: User Service (FastAPI - Python)

FastAPI is a lightweight, high-performance API framework for Python, perfect for microservices.

Step 1: Install FastAPI & Uvicorn
sh

```
pip install fastapi uvicorn
```

Step 2: Create user_service.py
python

```python
from fastapi import FastAPI

app = FastAPI()

users = [
    {"id": 1, "name": "Alice"},
    {"id": 2, "name": "Bob"}
]

@app.get("/users")
def get_users():
    return users

@app.get("/users/{user_id}")
def get_user(user_id: int):
    for user in users:
        if user["id"] == user_id:
            return user
    return {"error": "User not found"}
```

Step 3: Run the FastAPI Service

sh

```
uvicorn user_service:app --host 0.0.0.0 --port
8001 --reload
```

The API will be available at: http://localhost:8001/users

Microservice 2: Order Service (.NET Core Web API - C#)

.NET Core Web API is ideal for **enterprise-grade** microservices.

Step 1: Create a New ASP.NET Core Web API Project

sh

```
dotnet new webapi -n OrderService
cd OrderService
```

Step 2: Modify `Controllers/OrderController.cs`

csharp

```
using Microsoft.AspNetCore.Mvc;
using System.Collections.Generic;
```

```
[ApiController]
[Route("api/orders")]
public class OrderController : ControllerBase
{
    private static readonly List<object> Orders
= new List<object>
    {
        new { Id = 1, UserId = 1, Product =
"Laptop" },
        new { Id = 2, UserId = 2, Product =
"Phone" }
    };

    [HttpGet]
    public IActionResult GetOrders()
    {
        return Ok(Orders);
    }

    [HttpGet("{id}")]
    public IActionResult GetOrder(int id)
    {
        var order = Orders.Find(o =>
(int)o.GetType().GetProperty("Id").GetValue(o,
null) == id);
        return order == null ? NotFound() :
Ok(order);
    }
}
```

101

Step 3: Run the .NET Microservice

sh

```
dotnet run
```

The API will be available at:
`http://localhost:5000/api/orders`

Connecting Python & .NET Core Microservices

Calling the Python User API from .NET Core

Modify `OrderController.cs` to call the **FastAPI User Service**:

csharp

```csharp
using Microsoft.AspNetCore.Mvc;
using System.Net.Http;
using System.Threading.Tasks;

[ApiController]
[Route("api/orders")]
public class OrderController : ControllerBase
{
    private static readonly HttpClient client =
new HttpClient();
```

```
[HttpGet("user/{userId}")]
public        async        Task<IActionResult>
GetUserFromPythonService(int userId)
    {
        string            url            =
$"http://localhost:8001/users/{userId}";
        var        response      =        await
client.GetStringAsync(url);
        return Ok(response);
    }
}
```

Now, .NET Core can **fetch user details from the Python microservice**.

Containerizing Microservices with Docker

Each microservice runs independently, but **Docker** helps **package and deploy them efficiently**.

Step 1: Create Dockerfile for FastAPI Microservice

Create Dockerfile for Python Service

Dockerfile

```
FROM python:3.9
WORKDIR /app
 . /app
RUN pip install fastapi uvicorn
CMD ["uvicorn", "user_service:app", "--host",
"0.0.0.0", "--port", "8001"]
```

Build & Run the Container

sh

```
docker build -t user-service .
docker run -p 8001:8001 user-service
```

Step 2: Create Dockerfile for .NET Core Microservice

Create Dockerfile for .NET Core Service

Dockerfile

```
FROM mcr.microsoft.com/dotnet/aspnet:7.0
WORKDIR /app
 . /app
ENTRYPOINT ["dotnet", "OrderService.dll"]
```

Build & Run the Container

```sh
sh
```

```sh
docker build -t order-service .
docker run -p 5000:5000 order-service
```

Now, both microservices **run independently in Docker containers**.

Step 3: Running Services with Docker Compose

Create `docker-compose.yml` to run both services together:

```yaml
yaml

version: '3.8'

services:
  user-service:
    build: ./user_service
    ports:
      - "8001:8001"

  order-service:
    build: ./order_service
    ports:
```

```
- "5000:5000"
depends_on:
  - user-service
```

Start All Services

```sh
sh
```

```
docker-compose up --build
```

Now, both **FastAPI and .NET Core microservices** are running **in isolated containers**.

Conclusion: Why Microservices Make Cross-Platform Development Easier

Key Takeaways

Microservices break applications into smaller, independent services, making them **scalable and flexible**. **FastAPI (Python) & .NET Core** are **ideal choices** for cross-platform   microservices. **Docker enables seamless deployment**, ensuring each microservice runs in an isolated, scalable container.

106

Docker Compose manages multiple microservices efficiently.

Next Chapter: Serverless & Cloud-Native Cross-Platform Apps

CHAPTER 10

SERVERLESS & CLOUD-NATIVE CROSS-PLATFORM APPS

Serverless computing enables developers to **build, deploy, and scale applications** without managing the underlying infrastructure. This approach is cost-effective and ideal for **cross-platform applications**. In this chapter, we'll explore:

Using Azure Functions & AWS Lambda Deploying Python & C# Apps to the Cloud Reducing Infrastructure Costs with Serverless Computing

---

What is Serverless Computing?

Serverless computing allows applications to run in **event-driven, auto-scaled environments** where developers only pay for actual execution time. Unlike traditional cloud-based servers, there is **no need to manage virtual machines or containers**.

Benefits of Serverless Computing

No Server Management – Cloud providers handle infrastructure maintenance.

Auto-Scaling – Apps scale automatically based on traffic.

Cost-Effective – Pay only for execution time, not idle server usage.

Event-Driven Execution – Functions trigger based on HTTP requests, database changes, or cloud events.

Cross-Platform Flexibility – Python & .NET Core apps can run seamlessly in cloud environments.

Popular **serverless platforms** include:
AWS Lambda (Amazon Web Services)
Azure Functions (Microsoft Azure)
Google Cloud Functions

Using Azure Functions & AWS Lambda

What is AWS Lambda?

AWS Lambda is a **serverless compute service** that runs code **without provisioning servers**. Lambda functions are event-driven and support **Python, .NET Core, Node.js, and more**.

Deploying a Python Function in AWS Lambda

Step 1: Install AWS CLI & Serverless Framework

sh

```
pip install awscli
npm install -g serverless
```

Step 2: Create a Python Lambda Function

Create `lambda_function.py`

python

```
import json

def lambda_handler(event, context):
    return {
        "statusCode": 200,
        "body":  json.dumps({"message":  "Hello
from AWS Lambda!"})
    }
```

Step 3: Deploy to AWS

sh

```
serverless deploy
```

The function is now available on AWS.

What is Azure Functions?

Azure Functions allows you to **run event-driven serverless code** on the **Microsoft Azure cloud**. It supports **C#, Python, Java, and JavaScript**.

Deploying a C# Function in Azure Functions

Step 1: Install Azure CLI & Functions Core Tools

sh

```
npm install -g azure-functions-core-tools
az login
```

Step 2: Create an Azure Function

sh

```
func new --template "HttpTrigger" --name
MyFunction --language C#
```

Step 3: Modify the Function Code (MyFunction.cs)

csharp

```
using Microsoft.AspNetCore.Mvc;
using Microsoft.Azure.WebJobs;
using Microsoft.Azure.WebJobs.Extensions.Http;
```

```
using System.Threading.Tasks;

public static class MyFunction
{
    [FunctionName("MyFunction")]
    public static async Task<IActionResult> Run(

[HttpTrigger(AuthorizationLevel.Function,
"get")] string name)
    {
        return    new    OkObjectResult($"Hello
{name}, from Azure Functions!");
    }
}
```

Step 4: Deploy to Azure

```sh
sh
```

```
func azure functionapp publish MyAzureApp
```

The function is now running on Azure.

Deploying Python and C# Apps to the Cloud

Deploying a Python App on AWS Lambda

Step 1: Create a Flask API

```python
python
```

```
from flask import Flask, jsonify

app = Flask(__name__)

@app.route("/")
def home():
    return   jsonify({"message":   "Welcome   to
serverless Flask on AWS!"})

if __name__ == "__main__":
    app.run(debug=True)
```

Step 2: Deploy Using Serverless Framework

1. Install Serverless Framework:

   sh

   ```
   npm install -g serverless
   ```

2. Deploy to AWS:

   sh

   ```
   serverless deploy
   ```

The API is now live on AWS Lambda.

Deploying a .NET Core API on Azure Functions

Step 1: Create an ASP.NET Core Web API

sh

```
dotnet new webapi -n MyAzureApp
cd MyAzureApp
```

Step 2: Deploy to Azure

sh

```
az webapp up --name MyAzureApp --resource-group MyResourceGroup
```

The API is now live on **Azure App Services**.

Reducing Infrastructure Costs with Serverless Computing

Why Serverless is Cost-Effective

No Infrastructure Costs – No need to maintain virtual machines.

Pay-Per-Execution – Costs are based only on function execution   time.

114

Auto-Scaling Saves Costs – No need to pre-provision resources for high traffic.

Cloud Provider	Free Tier Allowance	Billing
AWS Lambda	1 million free requests/month	$0.20 per million requests
Azure Functions	1 million executions/month	$0.16 per million executions
Google Cloud Functions	2 million free executions/month	$0.40 per million

Example **Savings**

A traditional VM hosting a Python API **costs $20/month** even if idle.

A **serverless function only costs a few cents** when called.

Conclusion: Why Serverless is the Future of Cross-Platform Applications

Key Takeaways

Serverless computing eliminates server management, scaling automatically.

AWS Lambda & Azure Functions support Python & C# for cloud-native apps.

Deploying Python & .NET Core apps to the cloud is seamless and cost-effective.

Serverless solutions significantly reduce infrastructure costs.

Next Chapter: Scalability Strategies for High-Performance Apps (Load Balancing, Caching, and Optimizations)

PART 3

SECURITY, SCALABILITY & PERFORMANCE

CHAPTER 11

SECURITY BEST PRACTICES IN PYTHON & .NET CORE

Security is a **critical aspect** of modern applications, especially when dealing with **user authentication, data protection, and web vulnerabilities**. This chapter will cover:

Authentication & Authorization with OAuth, JWT
Preventing Common Vulnerabilities (SQL Injection, XSS,   CSRF)
Secure Coding Principles

Authentication & Authorization with OAuth, JWT

Authentication ensures **users are who they claim to be**, while authorization determines **what they can access**.

What is JWT (JSON Web Token)?

JWT (JSON Web Token) is a **compact, self-contained token** used for securely transmitting information between parties.

Stateless authentication (no need for session storage) **Signed with HMAC or RSA for security** **Widely used in RESTful APIs**

Implementing JWT in FastAPI (Python)

Step 1: Install Dependencies
sh

```
pip install fastapi[all] pyjwt
```
Step 2: Generate & Validate JWT Token
python

```
import jwt
from datetime import datetime, timedelta

SECRET_KEY = "mysecret"

# Function to create a token
def create_jwt(data: dict):
    expiration    =    datetime.utcnow()    +
timedelta(hours=1)
    data.update({"exp": expiration})
```

```
    return        jwt.encode(data,        SECRET_KEY,
algorithm="HS256")

# Function to decode a token
def verify_jwt(token: str):
    try:
        return    jwt.decode(token,    SECRET_KEY,
algorithms=["HS256"])
    except jwt.ExpiredSignatureError:
        return None
```

Now, FastAPI can authenticate users using JWT tokens.

Implementing JWT in ASP.NET Core (C#)

Step 1: Install Dependencies

sh

```
dotnet              add              package
Microsoft.AspNetCore.Authentication.JwtBearer
```

Step 2: Configure JWT Authentication (Startup.cs)

csharp

```
services.AddAuthentication(JwtBearerDefaults.Au
thenticationScheme)
    .AddJwtBearer(options =>
    {
```

```
options.RequireHttpsMetadata = false;
options.SaveToken = true;
options.TokenValidationParameters = new
TokenValidationParameters
    {
        ValidateIssuerSigningKey = true,
        IssuerSigningKey            =            new
SymmetricSecurityKey(Encoding.UTF8.GetBytes("my
secret")),
        ValidateIssuer = false,
        ValidateAudience = false
    };
});
```

JWT authentication is now enabled in .NET Core Web API.

What is OAuth 2.0?

OAuth 2.0 is an **industry-standard protocol** for secure API authorization.

Popular **OAuth** **providers**:

Google **OAuth**

Facebook **OAuth**

GitHub OAuth

Example: Google OAuth in FastAPI

```sh
sh

pip install authlib
python
```

```python
from       authlib.integrations.starlette_client
import OAuth

oauth = OAuth()
oauth.register(
    name="google",
    client_id="your-client-id",
    client_secret="your-client-secret",

access_token_url="https://accounts.google.com/o
/oauth2/token",

authorize_url="https://accounts.google.com/o/oa
uth2/auth",
)
```

Now, users can **log in with Google instead of using passwords**.

Preventing Common Vulnerabilities

SQL Injection (SQLi)

SQL Injection allows attackers to **manipulate database queries** through input fields.

Prevent SQL Injection in Python (Using Parameterized Queries)

python

```python
cursor.execute("SELECT * FROM users WHERE email = %s", (user_email,))
```

Prevent SQL Injection in .NET Core (Using Entity Framework)

csharp

```csharp
var user = dbContext.Users.SingleOrDefault(u => u.Email == email);
```

📖 **Never concatenate user input directly into SQL queries!**

Cross-Site Scripting (XSS)

XSS attacks allow injecting **malicious scripts** into web pages.

Prevent XSS in Python (Sanitize Input with Bleach)

```sh
pip install bleach
```

```python
import bleach
safe_input = bleach.clean(user_input)
```

Prevent XSS in .NET Core (Use Razor Encoding)

```html
@Html.Encode(userInput)
```

🚨 Always encode and sanitize user input!

Cross-Site Request Forgery (CSRF)

CSRF tricks users into performing **unintended actions** on authenticated sites.

Prevent CSRF in FastAPI

python

```
from    fastapi.middleware.trustedhost    import
TrustedHostMiddleware

app.add_middleware(TrustedHostMiddleware,
allowed_hosts=["mywebsite.com"])
```

Prevent CSRF in .NET Core (Use Anti-Forgery Tokens)

csharp

```
[ValidateAntiForgeryToken]
public IActionResult SecureAction() { }
```

📢 Use anti-CSRF tokens for form submissions!

Secure Coding Principles

Use   Environment   Variables   for   Secrets
Bad:

python

```
SECRET_KEY = "my_secret_key"
```

Good:

sh

```sh
export SECRET_KEY="my_secret_key"
```

Enable HTTPS in Web Applications

sh

```sh
dotnet dev-certs https --trust
```

Limit API Rate to Prevent Abuse
FastAPI (Using Starlette Middleware):

python

```python
from starlette.middleware.trustedhost import TrustedHostMiddleware

app.add_middleware(TrustedHostMiddleware, allowed_hosts=["*"])
```

Use Logging Instead of Printing Errors

python

```python
import logging

logging.error("Unauthorized access detected")
```

Conclusion: Securing Python & .NET Core Applications

Key Takeaways

Use JWT for secure authentication in Python & .NET Core.

OAuth 2.0 enables secure third-party authentication.
SQL Injection, XSS, and CSRF are major security threats that must be mitigated.
Secure coding practices (environment variables, HTTPS, logging) help prevent security risks.

Next Chapter: Scalability Strategies for High-Performance Apps (Load Balancing, Caching, and

CHAPTER 12

SCALABILITY STRATEGIES FOR HIGH-PERFORMANCE APPS

Scalability is critical for ensuring **fast, responsive, and reliable applications** as user traffic grows. In this chapter, we'll cover:

Load   Balancing   and   Caching   Techniques

Optimizing   Databases   for   Speed

Using Redis, RabbitMQ, and Other Tools

Load Balancing and Caching Techniques

What is Load Balancing?

Load balancing distributes incoming traffic across multiple servers   to:

Prevent   overload   on   a   single   server

Ensure   high   availability

Improve application performance

Load Balancing with Nginx

Nginx is a powerful **reverse proxy** that distributes requests across multiple backend servers.

Example Nginx Configuration for Load Balancing

Create /etc/nginx/nginx.conf:

```nginx

http {
    upstream backend_servers {
        server app1.example.com;
        server app2.example.com;
    }

    server {
        listen 80;
        location / {
            proxy_pass http://backend_servers;
        }
    }
}
```

Restart Nginx:

```sh

sudo systemctl restart nginx
```

129

Now, Nginx will distribute requests **evenly across multiple application servers**.

What is Caching?

Caching **stores frequently accessed data** to improve performance and reduce database load.

In-Memory Caching – Stores data in RAM for **fast access** (e.g., Redis, Memcached).
Page Caching – Stores entire HTML pages for **static content delivery**.
Query Caching – Caches **SQL query results** to reduce database queries.

Implementing Redis Caching in Python (FastAPI)

Install Redis:

```sh
pip install redis
```

Connect to Redis in FastAPI:

```python
```

```python
import redis

redis_client   =    redis.Redis(host="localhost",
port=6379, decode_responses=True)

def get_cached_data(key):
    data = redis_client.get(key)
    return data if data else None

def set_cached_data(key, value, expire=3600):
    redis_client.setex(key, expire, value)
```

This caches data for **faster API responses**.

Implementing Redis Caching in ASP.NET Core (C#)

Install Redis Package:

```sh
sh
```

```sh
dotnet add package StackExchange.Redis
```

Configure Redis in Startup.cs:

```csharp
csharp
```

```
services.AddStackExchangeRedisCache(options =>
{
    options.Configuration = "localhost:6379";
});
```

Use Redis for Caching:

```csharp
var cache = _cache.GetString("cachedData");
if (cache == null)
{
    _cache.SetString("cachedData",        "Hello,
Redis!", TimeSpan.FromMinutes(30));
}
```

Now, **Redis speeds up API calls** in .NET applications.

Optimizing Databases for Speed

Best Practices for Faster Databases

Indexing – Create indexes on frequently queried columns.

Partitioning – Split large tables into smaller chunks for efficiency.

Connection Pooling – Reduce the overhead of

opening/closing   connections.

Database Caching – Store query results in Redis.

Optimizing PostgreSQL Performance

Enable Indexing:

```sql
sql
```

```sql
CREATE INDEX idx_users_email ON users(email);
```

Enable   Connection   Pooling:
Install **PgBouncer** to manage **database connections efficiently**.

```sh
sh
```

```sh
sudo apt install pgbouncer
```

PostgreSQL is now optimized for high-traffic applications.

Optimizing MongoDB Performance

Create an Index for Faster Queries:

133

```sh
```

```
db.users.createIndex({ email: 1 })
```

Enable   Connection   Pooling:
Modify MongoDB **connection settings**:

```python
```

```
from pymongo import MongoClient

client                                    =
MongoClient("mongodb://localhost:27017",
maxPoolSize=100)
```

MongoDB queries are now much faster.

Using Redis, RabbitMQ, and Other Tools

Redis: High-Speed In-Memory Database

Stores **key-value pairs** in memory for **instant access**.
Used for **session storage, caching, and pub/sub messaging**.

Example: Redis for Session Storage (FastAPI)

```
python
```

```
session_token                              =
redis_client.set("session:12345",    "user_data",
ex=3600)
```

Example: Redis for Real-Time Chat (C# .NET Core)

```
csharp
```

```
await   _redis.PublishAsync("chat_channel",   "New
Message!");
```

RabbitMQ: Message Queue for Microservices

Handles **asynchronous message passing** between services. Prevents **data loss** and improves **fault tolerance**. Used in **event-driven architectures** (e.g., notifications, order processing).

Example: Sending Messages to RabbitMQ (Python)

```
python
```

```
import pika
```

```
connection                                  =
pika.BlockingConnection(pika.ConnectionParamete
rs("localhost"))
channel = connection.channel()

channel.queue_declare(queue="task_queue")

channel.basic_publish(exchange="",
routing_key="task_queue", body="New Task")
connection.close()
```

RabbitMQ ensures **messages are not lost if a service crashes**.

Implementing RabbitMQ in ASP.NET Core

Install RabbitMQ Client:

```sh
sh

dotnet add package RabbitMQ.Client
```

Publish a Message in C#

```csharp
csharp

using RabbitMQ.Client;
```

```
using System.Text;

var factory = new ConnectionFactory() { HostName
= "localhost" };
using         var         connection         =
factory.CreateConnection();
using var channel = connection.CreateModel();

channel.QueueDeclare(queue:        "task_queue",
durable: true, exclusive: false, autoDelete:
false);
var message = "New Task";
var body = Encoding.UTF8.GetBytes(message);

channel.BasicPublish(exchange: "", routingKey:
"task_queue", basicProperties: null, body:
body);
```

RabbitMQ now **sends and receives messages across services**.

Conclusion: Scaling Applications Efficiently

Key Takeaways

Load balancing distributes traffic **to prevent server overload**.

Redis caching improves API response times by storing frequently used data.

Database optimizations (indexing, connection pooling) improve query performance.

RabbitMQ helps **microservices communicate asynchronously**.

Next Chapter: Testing & Debugging Cross-Platform Applications

CHAPTER 13

TESTING & DEBUGGING CROSS-PLATFORM APPLICATIONS

Testing and debugging are essential for delivering **reliable, high-performance applications**. This chapter covers:

Unit Testing with PyTest & xUnit
Debugging Techniques in Python & C#
Performance Profiling Tools

Unit Testing with PyTest & xUnit

Why Unit Testing Matters?

Unit testing ensures that **each function, method, or module** in an application works as expected.

Detects bugs early before deployment.
Ensures code reliability and prevents regressions.
Automates testing in CI/CD pipelines.

Unit Testing in Python with PyTest

Step 1: Install PyTest

sh

```sh
pip install pytest
```

Step 2: Create a Python Function (app.py)

python

```python
def add_numbers(a, b):
    return a + b
```

Step 3: Write Unit Tests (test_app.py)

python

```python
from app import add_numbers

def test_add_numbers():
    assert add_numbers(2, 3) == 5
    assert add_numbers(-1, 1) == 0
```

Step 4: Run the Tests

sh

```sh
pytest
```

If all tests pass, PyTest shows:

```cpp
```

```
test_app.py::test_add_numbers PASSED
```

Unit Testing in C# with xUnit

Step 1: Install xUnit in .NET Core

```sh
```

```
dotnet add package xunit
```

Step 2: Create a C# Function (`Calculator.cs`)

```csharp
```

```
public class Calculator
{
    public int Add(int a, int b)
    {
        return a + b;
    }
}
```

Step 3: Write Unit Tests (`CalculatorTests.cs`)

141

```csharp

using Xunit;

public class CalculatorTests
{
    [Fact]
    public void TestAdd()
    {
        var calc = new Calculator();
        Assert.Equal(5, calc.Add(2, 3));
    }
}
```

Step 4: Run the Tests

```sh

dotnet test
```

Successful test output:

```
CalculatorTests.TestAdd PASSED
```

Debugging Techniques in Python & C#

Debugging Python Applications

142

Python provides several debugging tools for **troubleshooting runtime errors**.

Using Python's Built-in Debugger (pdb)

```python
import pdb

def divide(a, b):
    pdb.set_trace()  # Debugging starts here
    return a / b

divide(10, 0)
```

When this runs, it pauses execution and allows **step-by-step inspection**.

Using Debugging in VS Code

1. Open VS Code, select **Run → Start Debugging**.
2. Set **breakpoints** in the code.
3. Inspect variables, execution flow, and exceptions.

Debugging C# Applications in Visual Studio

Step 1: Set Breakpoints in Visual Studio

143

1. Open the C# project in **Visual Studio**.

2. Click the **left margin** next to a line of code to **set a breakpoint**.

3. Press **F5 (Start Debugging)** to run the app **in debug mode**.

Step 2: Inspect Variables

- Hover over variables to see **real-time values**.
- Use the **Watch Window** for deeper analysis.

Step 3: Using the Immediate Window

Run expressions to test outputs:

```scss
? myVariable
? myObject.MethodCall()
```

Visual Studio's Debugging Tools Help Detect & Fix Bugs Efficiently.

Performance Profiling Tools

Why Performance Profiling Matters?

Performance profiling helps **identify bottlenecks** in CPU, memory, and database usage.

Profiling Python Code with cProfile

```sh
python -m cProfile -s time app.py
```

cProfile analyzes execution time for each function.

Example: Profiling a Python Function

```python
import cProfile

def slow_function():
    sum([i**2 for i in range(1000000)])

cProfile.run('slow_function()')
```

This shows **how much time** is spent in each function.

Profiling .NET Core Applications

Using DotTrace (JetBrains)

- Install **DotTrace** from JetBrains.
- Attach it to a running .NET app.
- Analyze CPU/memory usage.

Using .NET's Built-in Profiling Tool

```sh

dotnet-trace collect --process-id <PID>
```

This collects **performance metrics for profiling**.

Conclusion: Ensuring Bug-Free, High-Performance Applications

Key Takeaways

PyTest (Python) & xUnit (.NET Core) provide efficient unit testing frameworks. **Debugging tools like pdb (Python) & Visual Studio Debugger (C#)** help troubleshoot issues. **Performance profiling tools (cProfile, dotnet-trace, DotTrace)** improve application efficiency.

Next Chapter: CI/CD for Cross-Platform Deployment

CHAPTER 14

CI/CD FOR CROSS-PLATFORM DEPLOYMENT

Continuous Integration and Continuous Deployment (**CI/CD**) automate the process of **building, testing, and deploying** applications, ensuring **faster, more reliable software delivery**. In this chapter, we'll cover:

Automating Builds with GitHub Actions & Azure DevOps
Writing Dockerfiles for Python & .NET Apps
Rolling Out Updates Safely

Automating Builds with GitHub Actions & Azure DevOps

CI/CD pipelines automatically **build, test, and deploy** applications when changes are pushed to a repository.

GitHub Actions: Automating CI/CD for Python & .NET

Step 1: Create a GitHub Actions Workflow for Python

Create `.github/workflows/python-ci.yml`:

```yaml
yaml

name: Python CI/CD Pipeline

on:
  push:
    branches:
      - main

jobs:
  build:
    runs-on: ubuntu-latest

    steps:
      - name: Checkout Repository
        uses: actions/checkout@v3

      - name: Set up Python
        uses: actions/setup-python@v3
        with:
          python-version: '3.9'

      - name: Install Dependencies
        run: pip install -r requirements.txt
```

149

```
- name: Run Tests
  run: pytest
```

Now, every push triggers tests before deployment.

Step 2: Create a GitHub Actions Workflow for .NET Core

Create `.github/workflows/dotnet-ci.yml`:

yaml

```
name: .NET Core CI/CD Pipeline

on:
  push:
    branches:
      - main

jobs:
  build:
    runs-on: ubuntu-latest

    steps:
      - name: Checkout Repository
        uses: actions/checkout@v3

      - name: Set up .NET
        uses: actions/setup-dotnet@v3
```

```
with:
    dotnet-version: '7.0'

    - name: Restore Dependencies
      run: dotnet restore

    - name: Build Application
      run:    dotnet    build    --configuration
Release

    - name: Run Tests
      run: dotnet test --configuration Release
```

This pipeline ensures that .NET apps are tested before deployment.

Azure DevOps: Automating CI/CD for Cloud Deployments

Azure DevOps supports **CI/CD pipelines** for **Python & .NET applications**.

Create a New Azure DevOps Pipeline
Sign in **to** Azure DevOps.
Create a **new** **pipeline**.

151

Select **GitHub** as the source. Add a pipeline **YAML file** (`azure-pipelines.yml`):

```yaml
trigger:
  - main

pool:
  vmImage: 'ubuntu-latest'

steps:
  - task: UsePythonVersion@0
    inputs:
      versionSpec: '3.9'

  - script: |
      pip install -r requirements.txt
      pytest
    displayName: 'Run Python Tests'

  - task: DotNetCoreCLI@2
    inputs:
      command: 'restore'

  - task: DotNetCoreCLI@2
    inputs:
      command: 'build'
      arguments: '--configuration Release'
```

```
- task: DotNetCoreCLI@2
  inputs:
    command: 'test'
    arguments: '--configuration Release'
```

Now, Azure DevOps will build and test Python & .NET apps automatically.

Writing Dockerfiles for Python & .NET Apps

What is Docker?

Docker **packages applications into containers**, making them portable across different platforms.

Runs anywhere (Windows, Linux, macOS, Cloud)
Isolates dependencies to prevent conflicts
Makes deployment easier

Writing a Dockerfile for a Python App

Create Dockerfile for a FastAPI App:

```
dockerfile
```

```
FROM python:3.9
WORKDIR /app
 . /app
RUN pip install -r requirements.txt
CMD ["uvicorn", "app:app", "--host", "0.0.0.0",
"--port", "8000"]
```

Build & Run the Container:

```
sh
```

```
docker build -t python-app .
docker run -p 8000:8000 python-app
```

Now, the Python application is running inside **a Docker container**.

Writing a Dockerfile for a .NET Core App

Create Dockerfile for .NET Core API:

```
dockerfile
```

```
FROM mcr.microsoft.com/dotnet/aspnet:7.0
WORKDIR /app
```

```
.  /app
RUN dotnet publish -c Release -o out
CMD ["dotnet", "/app/out/MyApp.dll"]
```

Build & Run the Container:

```sh
```

```
docker build -t dotnet-app .
docker run -p 5000:5000 dotnet-app
```

The .NET Core API is now running inside a container.

Rolling Out Updates Safely

Strategies for Safe Deployments

Blue-Green Deployment – Deploy a new version while keeping the old version live.

Canary Deployment – Release new versions **gradually** to a subset of users.

Feature Flags – Enable/disable new features **without redeploying**.

Rolling Updates – Update one instance at a time **to avoid downtime**.

155

Blue-Green Deployment in Kubernetes

Create a Kubernetes Deployment (`deployment.yaml`)

yaml

```yaml
apiVersion: apps/v1
kind: Deployment
metadata:
  name: myapp
spec:
  replicas: 2
  selector:
    matchLabels:
      app: myapp
  template:
    metadata:
      labels:
        app: myapp
    spec:
      containers:
      - name: myapp
        image: myapp:v2
```

Apply the Deployment:

sh

```
kubectl apply -f deployment.yaml
```

The new version is deployed while the old one is still running.

Rolling Updates in Docker Compose

Create `docker-compose.yml` for Rolling Updates:

```yaml
yaml

version: '3'
services:
  web:
    image: myapp:v2
    ports:
      - "80:80"
    deploy:
      update_config:
        order: start-first
```

Deploy the New Version Safely:

```sh
sh

docker-compose up -d
```

157

This updates the service while keeping the old version live.

Conclusion: Automating Deployment for Reliability & Scalability

Key Takeaways

GitHub Actions & Azure DevOps automate builds & testing for Python & .NET.
Docker allows seamless deployment of cross-platform apps.
Blue-Green & Canary deployments prevent downtime.
Rolling updates deploy changes safely without affecting users.

Next Chapter: Integrating AI & Machine Learning in Cross-Platform Apps

CHAPTER 15

INTEGRATING AI & MACHINE LEARNING IN CROSS-PLATFORM APPS

AI and machine learning (ML) are transforming **modern applications**, enabling intelligent automation, predictions, and data-driven decision-making. This chapter explores:

Using Python ML Libraries (TensorFlow, Scikit-learn) Integrating AI into .NET Apps with ML.NET Practical Examples

Using Python ML Libraries (TensorFlow, Scikit-learn)

Python dominates **machine learning and AI** due to its rich ecosystem of libraries, including **TensorFlow, PyTorch, and Scikit-learn**.

Why Use Python for AI?

Massive ML ecosystem (TensorFlow, Scikit-learn, Pandas, NumPy)

Pre-trained models available for quick integration

Cross-platform support (Windows, macOS, Linux)

Seamless integration with .NET using **Python.NET and REST APIs**

Using Scikit-learn for Basic ML in Python

Scikit-learn is ideal for **traditional ML models** like regression, classification, and clustering.

Step 1: Install Dependencies

```sh

pip install scikit-learn pandas numpy
```

Step 2: Train a Simple Machine Learning Model

```python

import numpy as np
import pandas as pd
from          sklearn.model_selection          import
train_test_split
```

```python
from        sklearn.linear_model         import
LinearRegression

# Sample dataset
data = {"Experience": [1, 3, 5, 7, 9], "Salary":
[30000, 40000, 50000, 60000, 70000]}
df = pd.DataFrame(data)

# Split data into training and testing sets
X = df[["Experience"]]
y = df["Salary"]
X_train,   X_test,   y_train,   y_test   =
train_test_split(X, y, test_size=0.2)

# Train a Linear Regression Model
model = LinearRegression()
model.fit(X_train, y_train)

# Predict Salary
exp = np.array([[6]])
predicted_salary = model.predict(exp)
print(f"Predicted   Salary   for   6   years   of
experience: ${predicted_salary[0]:,.2f}")
```

The model **predicts salary** based on experience using **linear regression**.

Using TensorFlow for Deep Learning in Python

Step 1: Install TensorFlow

sh

```sh
pip install tensorflow
```

Step 2: Train a Neural Network for Image Recognition

python

```python
import tensorflow as tf
from tensorflow import keras

# Define a simple Neural Network
model = keras.Sequential([
    keras.layers.Dense(64,    activation="relu",
input_shape=(10,)),
    keras.layers.Dense(32, activation="relu"),
    keras.layers.Dense(1, activation="sigmoid")
])

# Compile the model
model.compile(optimizer="adam",
loss="binary_crossentropy",
metrics=["accuracy"])
```

TensorFlow enables **deep learning** models for **image recognition, NLP, and predictive analytics**.

Integrating AI into .NET Apps with ML.NET

What is ML.NET?

ML.NET is Microsoft's **machine learning framework** for .NET developers.

Train and deploy ML models in C# Supports regression, classification, and recommendations
Works with .NET Core and .NET 7+
Uses ONNX to import pre-trained models from Python

Installing ML.NET

```sh

dotnet add package Microsoft.ML
```

Training a Machine Learning Model in .NET Core

Step 1: Define a Data Model (HouseData.cs)

csharp

```csharp
public class HouseData
{
    public float Size { get; set; }
    public float Price { get; set; }
}
```

Step 2: Train a Regression Model (Program.cs)

csharp

```csharp
using System;
using Microsoft.ML;
using Microsoft.ML.Data;

class Program
{
    static void Main()
    {
        var context = new MLContext();

        var data = new[]
        {
```

```
        new HouseData { Size = 1000, Price =
200000 },
        new HouseData { Size = 1500, Price =
250000 },
        new HouseData { Size = 2000, Price =
300000 },
    };

    var          dataView          =
context.Data.LoadFromEnumerable(data);

    var          pipeline          =
context.Transforms.Concatenate("Features", new[]
{ "Size" })

.Append(context.Regression.Trainers.Sdca(labelC
olumnName: "Price"));

    var model = pipeline.Fit(dataView);

    var          predictionEngine          =
context.Model.CreatePredictionEngine<HouseData,
PricePrediction>(model);
    var          prediction          =
predictionEngine.Predict(new HouseData { Size =
1800 });

    Console.WriteLine($"Predicted price  for
1800 sqft house: ${prediction.Price:0.00}");
```

165

```
    }
}

public class PricePrediction
{
    [ColumnName("Score")]
    public float Price { get; set; }
}
```

ML.NET predicts house prices based on size.

Practical Examples of AI in Cross-Platform Apps

Example 1: Using Python AI in a .NET App via REST API

Python can **train and serve ML models**, while .NET can **consume AI predictions**.

Step 1: Expose a FastAPI ML Model

```python
from fastapi import FastAPI
from        sklearn.linear_model        import
LinearRegression
```

166

```python
app = FastAPI()

model = LinearRegression()
model.fit([[1], [3], [5], [7]], [1000, 3000, 5000, 7000])

@app.get("/predict")
def predict(experience: int):
    return                  {"predicted_salary":
model.predict([[experience]])[0]}
```

Step 2: Call the API in a .NET Core App

```csharp
csharp

using System;
using System.Net.Http;
using System.Threading.Tasks;

class Program
{
    static async Task Main()
    {
        using var client = new HttpClient();
        var         response      =         await
client.GetStringAsync("http://localhost:8000/pr
edict?experience=6");
        Console.WriteLine($"Predicted    Salary:
{response}");
    }
```

167

```
}
```

Now, a .NET application **fetches ML predictions from a Python backend**.

Example 2: Using ML.NET Inside a Blazor App

ML.NET can be used inside a **Blazor UI application** for **real-time predictions**.

Step 1: Create a Blazor Page (`Predict.razor`)

razor

```razor
@page "/predict"
@inject PredictionService PredictionService

<h3>Predict House Price</h3>
<input type="number" @bind="houseSize" />
<button
@onclick="MakePrediction">Predict</button>
<p>Predicted Price: @prediction</p>

@code {
    private float houseSize;
    private float prediction;
```

```csharp
    private void MakePrediction()
    {
        prediction                              =
PredictionService.PredictPrice(houseSize);
    }
}
```

Step 2: Define the Prediction Service (`PredictionService.cs`)

csharp

```csharp
public class PredictionService
{
    private readonly PredictionEngine<HouseData,
PricePrediction> _predictionEngine;

    public PredictionService()
    {
        var mlContext = new MLContext();
        var model = mlContext.Model.Load("house-
price-model.zip", out _);
        _predictionEngine                       =
mlContext.Model.CreatePredictionEngine<HouseDat
a, PricePrediction>(model);
    }

    public float PredictPrice(float size)
    {
```

169

```
      return        _predictionEngine.Predict(new
HouseData { Size = size }).Price;
    }
}
```

Now, **Blazor predicts house prices** using **ML.NET in a browser**.

Conclusion: Making Cross-Platform Apps Intelligent

Key Takeaways

Python excels in AI & ML, with **TensorFlow and Scikit-learn** for deep learning.
ML.NET brings machine learning to .NET Core applications.
Python-based AI models can be integrated into .NET apps via REST APIs.
AI-powered Blazor apps enable real-time machine learning predictions.

Next Chapter: Building Desktop Apps with .NET & Python (PyQt, Electron.NET, and MAUI)

CHAPTER 16

BUILDING DESKTOP APPS WITH .NET & PYTHON

Building **cross-platform desktop applications** requires frameworks that allow for **native performance** while supporting **multiple operating systems**. In this chapter, we'll explore:

Developing Cross-Platform Desktop Apps Using PyQt, Electron.NET

When to Use Python GUI Frameworks vs. .NET Core Frameworks

Developing Cross-Platform Desktop Apps Using PyQt, Electron.NET

What is PyQt?

PyQt is a **set of Python bindings for Qt**, a popular C++ framework used for creating **graphical user interfaces**

(GUIs). It is ideal for building **cross-platform desktop apps** for Windows, macOS, and Linux.

Powerful, full-featured GUI toolkit

Supports Qt Widgets, OpenGL, and WebKit

Can create both simple and complex UIs

Developing a Simple PyQt Desktop App

Install PyQt5

```sh
sh
```

```
pip install pyqt5
```

Create a Basic PyQt App

```python
python
```

```python
import sys
from PyQt5.QtWidgets import QApplication,
QWidget, QLabel, QVBoxLayout

class App(QWidget):
    def __init__(self):
        super().__init__()
        self.setWindowTitle('PyQt Example')

        # Layout and Label
```

```
        layout = QVBoxLayout()
        label = QLabel('Hello, PyQt!')
        layout.addWidget(label)

        self.setLayout(layout)
        self.show()

# Run the app
app = QApplication(sys.argv)
window = App()
sys.exit(app.exec_())
```

Run the App

```sh
sh
```

```
python app.py
```

The app opens a window displaying "Hello, PyQt!". PyQt enables building **rich, native-like applications** that run on multiple platforms.

What is Electron.NET?

Electron.NET is a framework that allows you to build **cross-platform desktop apps** using **.NET Core** and **web technologies** (HTML, CSS, JavaScript). Electron apps run within a **webview** and access native OS functionality via APIs.

Web technologies for the UI (HTML, CSS, JS) .NET Core for backend logic Cross-platform (Windows, macOS, Linux) Ideal for apps that need web-like functionality with native performance

Setting Up Electron.NET

Install Electron.NET CLI

```sh
```

```sh
dotnet tool install ElectronNET.CLI -g
```

Create a New Electron.NET Project

```sh
```

```sh
dotnet new electronnet -o MyElectronApp
cd MyElectronApp
```

Run the Electron App

```sh
```

```sh
electronize start
```

Electron.NET will open the app in a **native window**, running HTML/JavaScript inside it.

When to Use Python GUI Frameworks vs. .NET Core Frameworks

Both **Python** and **.NET Core** provide frameworks to build cross-platform desktop apps. The choice depends on **use case, performance requirements**, and **developer familiarity**.

When to Use Python GUI Frameworks (e.g., PyQt, Kivy, Tkinter)

Best for Rapid Development and Prototyping

- Python's simplicity allows for **quick prototyping** of desktop apps.
- **PyQt** is powerful for creating feature-rich applications with **native look and feel**.
- **Tkinter** and **Kivy** are good for building **simple apps** quickly.

Best for Data Science and Scientific Applications

- Python is widely used in **data science, AI**, and **machine learning**.
- Use Python-based frameworks when you need to integrate with **data analysis** libraries like **Pandas, NumPy**, or **SciPy**.
- **Kivy** is a great choice for **mobile apps** with Python as well.

Best for Simplicity

- **Kivy** and **Tkinter** are simple to use and ideal for apps that don't need complex UI components.
- **PyQt** is better for **large, production-level applications**, but still maintains ease of use compared to .NET Core frameworks.

When to Use .NET Core Frameworks (e.g., WPF, MAUI, Avalonia)

Best for Performance-Critical Applications

- **.NET Core** is compiled, offering better **performance** compared to Python-based GUI frameworks.

- Ideal for **enterprise-level applications** where performance is critical.
- **WPF** (Windows Presentation Foundation) and **.NET MAUI** are perfect for **native UI** and **high-performance desktop apps**.

Best for Enterprise Applications

- If you're already working in the **Microsoft ecosystem**, .NET Core frameworks are a natural fit.
- .NET's integration with tools like **Azure, SQL Server**, and **Active Directory** makes it ideal for enterprise apps.

Best for Rich Desktop UIs

- **WPF** offers **advanced data binding** and **graphics capabilities**, making it great for building **feature-rich desktop applications**.
- **.NET MAUI** is a **unified framework** for building mobile and desktop applications, replacing Xamarin.

Comparison: Python GUI Frameworks vs. .NET Core Frameworks

Feature	Python GUI Frameworks	.NET Core Frameworks
Ease of Use	Simple & fast for prototyping	Moderate, but powerful for larger apps
Performance	Slower due to interpreted nature	Faster due to compiled code
Cross-Platform	Yes (PyQt, Kivy, Tkinter)	Yes (WPF, MAUI, Avalonia)
UI Flexibility	High (PyQt, Kivy)	High (WPF, MAUI)
Best For	Prototyping, data science, simple apps	Enterprise apps, high-performance apps, rich UIs
Integration	Great with Python data science tools	Excellent with .NET ecosystem, including cloud and databases

Conclusion: Choosing the Right Framework for Desktop Development

Key Takeaways

PyQt and **Kivy** are great for **rapid development** and **data-centric applications** in Python.
Electron.NET is ideal for **cross-platform apps using web technologies** and **.NET Core**.
WPF and **.NET MAUI** are more suitable for **performance-critical** and **enterprise-grade applications** in the .NET ecosystem.

Next Chapter: Serverless & Cloud-Native Cross-Platform Apps

179

CHAPTER 17

MOBILE DEVELOPMENT WITH PYTHON & C#

In today's world, developing **mobile applications** that can run on both **Android and iOS** with a single codebase is crucial. This chapter will guide you through:

Using Kivy (Python) vs. Xamarin/.NET MAUI

Creating Android & iOS Apps with a Single Codebase

Using Kivy (Python) vs. Xamarin/.NET MAUI

What is Kivy?

Kivy is an open-source Python library for **building multi-touch applications**. It's great for **cross-platform mobile** development, allowing you to create apps for **Android, iOS, Linux, macOS**, and **Windows** using a single codebase.

Cross-Platform – Supports **Android, iOS, Linux, macOS, and** **Windows**.

Flexible UI – Provides customizable UI elements for building **mobile** **apps**.
Ideal for Prototyping & Small Apps – Great for **rapid prototyping** and simple mobile apps.

Setting Up Kivy for Android/iOS Development

Install Kivy:

```sh
```

```
pip install kivy
```

Create a Simple Kivy App

```python
```

```
from kivy.app import App
from kivy.uix.button import Button

class MyApp(App):
    def build(self):
        return Button(text="Hello, Kivy!")

if __name__ == "__main__":
    MyApp().run()
```

Run the App (on desktop)

```sh
sh
```

```
python main.py
```

Deploying to Android/iOS requires setting up **Kivy's Buildozer (Android)** or **Xcode (iOS)**.

What is Xamarin?

Xamarin (part of the .NET ecosystem) allows you to create **native mobile apps** for Android and iOS using **C#**. Xamarin provides **native performance** while sharing a significant portion of the codebase between platforms.

Native Performance – Xamarin apps run with **native performance** on both Android and iOS. **.NET Integration** – Works seamlessly with the **.NET ecosystem** (Azure, SQL Server, etc.). **Great for Enterprise Apps** – Ideal for **large-scale mobile apps**.

Setting Up Xamarin for Mobile Development

Install Xamarin via Visual Studio. Create a New Xamarin Project in Visual Studio (Android

&   iOS).

Write Cross-Platform Code

```csharp
public class App : Application
{
    public App()
    {
        MainPage = new ContentPage
        {
            Content = new Button
            {
                Text = "Hello, Xamarin!"
            }
        };
    }
}
```

Deploy to Android/iOS directly from Visual Studio.

What is .NET MAUI?

.NET MAUI (Multi-platform App UI) is the **next evolution of Xamarin** for building cross-platform mobile apps. It

183

simplifies building apps that run on **Android, iOS, macOS, and Windows** with a **single codebase**.

Unified Codebase – Works across **Android, iOS, macOS, and** **Windows**.

Native Performance – Provides **native UI components** on each platform.

Cross-Platform UI – Supports building **rich, modern UIs**.

Setting Up .NET MAUI for Mobile Development

Install Visual Studio 2022 with the **.NET MAUI** workload. **Create a New .NET MAUI Project:**

```sh
```

```sh
dotnet new maui -n MyMAUIApp
```

Write Cross-Platform Code (same as Xamarin, but with simplified controls and UI elements).

```csharp

public class MainPage : ContentPage
{
    public MainPage()
    {
```

```
        var label = new Label { Text = "Hello,
.NET MAUI!" };
        var button = new Button { Text = "Click
Me" };
        button.Clicked += (s, e) => label.Text =
"Button clicked!";

        Content = new StackLayout { Children = {
label, button } };
    }
}
```

Run and Deploy to Android/iOS, macOS, or Windows directly from Visual Studio.

Creating Android & iOS Apps with a Single Codebase

Both **Kivy** and **Xamarin/.NET MAUI** enable **cross-platform development**, but the choice depends on **project requirements, language preference**, and **platform integration needs**.

When to Use Kivy for Mobile Development

Prototyping – Kivy is great for **rapid development** and **prototyping** small to medium-sized apps.

Python Ecosystem – If you need to integrate with Python libraries for **data science**, **machine learning**, or **IoT**, Kivy is a strong choice.

Non-Native UIs – For apps with **custom UIs** and simpler design, Kivy works well.

Kivy Example: Building a Simple Mobile App

```python
from kivy.app import App
from kivy.uix.button import Button

class MyApp(App):
    def build(self):
        return Button(text="Hello, Kivy!")

if __name__ == "__main__":
    MyApp().run()
```

Deploying the app for **Android** involves using **Buildozer**, and for **iOS**, you'll need **Xcode**.

When to Use Xamarin/.NET MAUI for Mobile Development

Enterprise-Grade Apps – Xamarin and .NET MAUI are best for **large-scale mobile applications** with **native performance** and **complex UIs**.

.NET Ecosystem – If you're already working within the **.NET** or **Microsoft ecosystem**, **Xamarin** and **.NET MAUI** integrate seamlessly.

Access to Native Features – Xamarin and MAUI offer easy access to **native device features** (camera, GPS, sensors, etc.).

Xamarin/.NET MAUI Example: Simple Cross-Platform App

```csharp
public class MainPage : ContentPage
{
    public MainPage()
    {
        var label = new Label { Text = "Hello,
Xamarin/.NET MAUI!" };
        var button = new Button { Text = "Click
Me" };
        button.Clicked += (s, e) => label.Text =
"Button clicked!";

        Content = new StackLayout { Children = {
label, button } };
    }
}
```

Conclusion: Choosing the Right Framework for Mobile Development

Key Takeaways

Kivy is great for **prototyping and simple apps**, especially when leveraging the **Python ecosystem**. **Xamarin** and **.NET MAUI** are ideal for **high-performance, native mobile apps**, with **seamless .NET integration**.

Xamarin/.NET MAUI offer **native UI components** and are better for **enterprise-level apps**. **Kivy** excels in **cross-platform support** with a **lightweight approach** for mobile apps.

Next Chapter: Real-World Project: Building a Cross-Platform App with Python & .NET MAUI

CHAPTER 18

IOT & EMBEDDED SYSTEMS WITH PYTHON & .NET CORE

The **Internet of Things (IoT)** and **embedded systems** are revolutionizing the way we interact with technology. In this chapter, we'll explore how to connect **IoT devices** using **Python** and **.NET Core**, and implement **Raspberry Pi** and **Arduino** projects for real-world applications.

Connecting IoT Devices Using Python & .NET Core

Implementing Raspberry Pi and Arduino Projects

Connecting IoT Devices Using Python & .NET Core

Both **Python** and **.NET Core** offer great tools for working with **IoT devices**, allowing you to easily connect sensors, collect data, and control hardware.

Python for IoT

Python is widely used in the **IoT community** because of its simplicity, flexibility, and the vast number of libraries available for interacting with sensors and devices.

Setting Up Python for IoT Development

To work with IoT devices, such as sensors or Raspberry Pi, you'll need libraries like **RPi.GPIO** (for Raspberry Pi) or **Adafruit CircuitPython** (for various sensors).

Install Raspberry Pi Libraries (RPi.GPIO)

sh

```
pip install RPi.GPIO
```

Simple GPIO Example (Blinking an LED on Raspberry Pi)

python

```
import RPi.GPIO as GPIO
import time

# Set up the GPIO pin
GPIO.setmode(GPIO.BCM)
GPIO.setup(18, GPIO.OUT)
```

```
# Blink LED
while True:
    GPIO.output(18, GPIO.HIGH)   # Turn LED on
    time.sleep(1)
    GPIO.output(18, GPIO.LOW)    # Turn LED off
    time.sleep(1)
```

Running   **the**   **Script**

Run the script on your Raspberry Pi:

```sh
sh
```

```
python led_blink.py
```

This will blink an **LED** on GPIO pin **18**.

Working with Sensors

Python is also used to read data from sensors like temperature, humidity, and motion sensors.

Example: Reading temperature using **DHT11** sensor and **Adafruit's CircuitPython DHT** library.

```sh
sh
```

```
pip install adafruit-circuitpython-dht
python
```

```
import adafruit_dht
import board

dhtDevice = adafruit_dht.DHT11(board.D4)   # GPIO
pin D4 for the sensor

try:
    temperature = dhtDevice.temperature
    humidity = dhtDevice.humidity
    print(f"Temperature:           {temperature}C
Humidity: {humidity}%")
except RuntimeError as error:
    print(error)
```

This script reads the **temperature and humidity** from a connected DHT11 sensor.

.NET Core for IoT

.NET Core, with its **cross-platform** capabilities, is also an excellent choice for IoT applications. **.NET IoT libraries** allow you to interact with devices like Raspberry Pi, Arduino, and other sensors.

Setting Up .NET Core for IoT Development

Install the .NET IoT Libraries

```sh
```

```sh
dotnet add package System.Device.Gpio
```

Control GPIO Pins on Raspberry Pi (Blinking an LED)

```csharp
```

```csharp
using System;
using System.Device.Gpio;
using System.Threading;

class Program
{
    static void Main()
    {
        using var controller = new GpioController();
        const int ledPin = 18;
        controller.OpenPin(ledPin, PinMode.Output);

        while (true)
        {
            controller.Write(ledPin, PinValue.High); // Turn LED on
```

193

```
        Thread.Sleep(1000);
        controller.Write(ledPin,
PinValue.Low);  // Turn LED off
        Thread.Sleep(1000);
      }
    }
}
```

Running   the   .NET   Core   IoT   App

Run the app on your Raspberry Pi with:

```sh
```

```
dotnet run
```

This will blink an **LED** on GPIO pin **18** on the Raspberry Pi.

Reading Data from Sensors (e.g., Temperature)

You can also use **.NET Core** to read data from various sensors like **temperature, humidity**, or **motion**.

For example, with a **DHT11 sensor** and the appropriate driver, you can read temperature data into your .NET application.

Implementing Raspberry Pi and Arduino Projects

Raspberry Pi Projects with Python & .NET Core

Raspberry Pi is a **small, affordable computer** that supports both Python and .NET Core for IoT applications. Let's explore a couple of interesting projects.

Building a Temperature and Humidity Monitor

Using Python or .NET Core, you can **interface with the DHT11 sensor** to monitor the **temperature and humidity** in a room.

Python Example with DHT11 Sensor
Follow the same example from earlier, using the **DHT11** sensor to read data and display it on the console.

.NET Core Example with DHT11 Sensor
For .NET Core, you can use the **System.Device.Gpio** package to interact with the sensor and display the data in the terminal.

Creating a Motion Detector

You can use a **PIR (Passive Infrared)** sensor to detect motion. Both **Python** and **.NET Core** can handle the GPIO pin reads to activate the motion detection.

- In **Python**, use **RPi.GPIO** to read the PIR sensor's signal and trigger an action.
- In **.NET Core**, use **System.Device.Gpio** to handle the logic and trigger events on motion detection.

Arduino Projects with Python & .NET Core

Arduino is a **microcontroller platform** widely used in IoT projects. While **Arduino sketches** are primarily written in C/C++, you can interface Arduino with **Python** and **.NET Core** for enhanced functionalities.

Controlling an LED with Arduino and Python

Set up the Arduino to turn on/off an LED with a basic sketch:

cpp

```
void setup() {
```

196

```
  pinMode(13, OUTPUT);  // Set pin 13 to output
}

void loop() {
  digitalWrite(13, HIGH);  // Turn LED on
  delay(1000);
  digitalWrite(13, LOW);   // Turn LED off
  delay(1000);
}
```

Python to Control Arduino via Serial Communication

You can use **PySerial** to communicate with the Arduino over USB and send commands to control the LED.

```sh
sh

pip install pyserial
python

import serial
import time

arduino = serial.Serial('COM3', 9600)  # Change
COM port accordingly

while True:
    arduino.write(b'1')  # Send command to turn
LED on
    time.sleep(1)
```

```
    arduino.write(b'0')   # Send command to turn
LED off
    time.sleep(1)
```

Controlling Arduino from .NET Core

You can use **System.IO.Ports** in .NET Core to **read and write** data to Arduino over the serial port.

```csharp
using System.IO.Ports;

class Program
{
    static void Main()
    {
        SerialPort        arduino        =        new
SerialPort("COM3", 9600);
        arduino.Open();

        while (true)
        {
            arduino.WriteLine("1");    //    Send
command to Arduino to turn LED on
            Thread.Sleep(1000);
            arduino.WriteLine("0");    //    Send
command to turn LED off
            Thread.Sleep(1000);
        }
```

```
      }
}
```

Conclusion: Connecting IoT Devices and Building Embedded Systems

Key Takeaways

Python is ideal for **rapid development** of IoT projects, with libraries like **RPi.GPIO** and **Adafruit CircuitPython**. **.NET Core** offers **native performance** for IoT applications using libraries like **System.Device.Gpio** and **ML.NET**. **Raspberry Pi and Arduino** are perfect platforms for **real-world IoT applications**. Python and .NET Core can both **interface with sensors, control hardware**, and **build complex IoT systems**.

Next Chapter: Edge Computing with Python & .NET Core

CHAPTER 19

BLOCKCHAIN & CROSS-PLATFORM DEVELOPMENT

Blockchain technology is transforming industries by enabling **decentralized applications** (DApps), **secure transactions**, and **smart contracts**. In this chapter, we'll explore how to write **blockchain applications** using **Python** and **C#**, and understand the development of **smart contracts** and **decentralized applications**.

Writing Blockchain Applications with Python & C# Smart Contracts and Decentralized Applications (DApps)

Writing Blockchain Applications with Python & C#

Blockchain Basics

At a high level, a **blockchain** is a **distributed ledger** that securely records transactions in **blocks**. These blocks are linked together to form a chain, which ensures that no data is tampered with.

A blockchain system includes the following key components:

- **Nodes**: Participants in the network who validate transactions.
- **Ledger**: A list of all transactions in blocks.
- **Consensus Mechanism**: A protocol that helps the network agree on the state of the ledger.
- **Cryptography**: Ensures that transactions are secure and identities are protected.

Blockchain with Python

Python is a **popular choice** for building **blockchain applications** due to its simplicity, wide array of libraries, and integration with other tools.

Building a Simple Blockchain in Python

Install **Dependencies**
While this is a basic implementation, you might need libraries like **Flask** and **hashlib** for creating APIs and generating cryptographic hashes.

```sh
pip install Flask hashlib
```

Write a Simple Blockchain in Python

```python
import hashlib
import time
import json

class Block:
    def __init__(self, index, timestamp, data, previous_hash):
        self.index = index
        self.timestamp = timestamp
        self.data = data
        self.previous_hash = previous_hash
        self.hash = self.calculate_hash()

    def calculate_hash(self):
        block_string = str(self.index) + self.timestamp + str(self.data) + self.previous_hash
        return hashlib.sha256(block_string.encode('utf-8')).hexdigest()

def create_genesis_block():
```

```
    return    Block(0,    time.strftime("%Y-%m-%d
%H:%M:%S"), "Genesis Block", "0")

def create_new_block(previous_block, data):
    index = previous_block.index + 1
    timestamp    =    time.strftime("%Y-%m-%d
%H:%M:%S")
    return    Block(index,    timestamp,    data,
previous_block.hash)

blockchain = [create_genesis_block()]
previous_block = blockchain[0]

for i in range(1, 10):
    new_block = create_new_block(previous_block,
f"Block {i} data")
    blockchain.append(new_block)
    previous_block = new_block
    print(f"Block #{new_block.index}  has  been
added to the blockchain!")
    print(f"Hash: {new_block.hash}\n")
```

This Python script creates a simple blockchain and prints out the **block index**, **data**, and **hash**.

Blockchain with C#

C# can also be used to build blockchain applications, with libraries like **NBitcoin** (for Bitcoin-related blockchain development) and **blockchain.net** for general blockchain apps.

Setting Up a Simple Blockchain in C#

Install **Dependencies**:
To get started with blockchain development in C#, you'll need to install libraries such as **NBitcoin** for Bitcoin-based development.

sh

```
dotnet add package NBitcoin
```

Create a Simple Blockchain App in C#

csharp

```
using System;
using System.Security.Cryptography;
using System.Text;

public class Block
{
    public int Index { get; set; }
    public string Timestamp { get; set; }
```

204

```csharp
    public string Data { get; set; }
    public string PreviousHash { get; set; }
    public string Hash { get; set; }

    public Block(int index, string timestamp,
string data, string previousHash)
    {
        Index = index;
        Timestamp = timestamp;
        Data = data;
        PreviousHash = previousHash;
        Hash = CalculateHash();
    }


    public string CalculateHash()
    {
        string             blockData           =
$"{Index}{Timestamp}{Data}{PreviousHash}";
        using (SHA256 sha256 = SHA256.Create())
        {
            byte[]          hashBytes           =
sha256.ComputeHash(Encoding.UTF8.GetBytes(block
Data));
            return
BitConverter.ToString(hashBytes).Replace("-",
"").ToLower();
        }
    }
}
```

205

```
public class Blockchain
{
    public static Block CreateGenesisBlock()
    {
        return           new           Block(0,
DateTime.UtcNow.ToString(),    "Genesis    Block",
"0");
    }

    public   static   Block   CreateNewBlock(Block
previousBlock, string data)
    {
        int index = previousBlock.Index + 1;
        string              timestamp              =
DateTime.UtcNow.ToString();
        return new Block(index, timestamp, data,
previousBlock.Hash);
    }
}

class Program
{
    static void Main(string[] args)
    {
        Blockchain    blockchain    =    new
Blockchain();
        Block            genesisBlock            =
Blockchain.CreateGenesisBlock();
```

206

```
Block previousBlock = genesisBlock;

for (int i = 1; i <= 5; i++)
{
    Block         newBlock         =
Blockchain.CreateNewBlock(previousBlock, $"Block
{i} data");
    Console.WriteLine($"Block
#{newBlock.Index}  has  been  added  to  the
blockchain!");
    Console.WriteLine($"Hash:
{newBlock.Hash}\n");
    previousBlock = newBlock;
    }
}
}
```

This C# code simulates a **blockchain structure**, and generates blocks with **timestamp** and **data**.

Smart Contracts and Decentralized Applications (DApps)

What Are Smart Contracts?

Smart contracts are self-executing contracts with the terms of the agreement directly written into code. They are typically used in **blockchain-based applications**, enabling **trustless transactions**.

Executed automatically when predefined conditions are met.

Eliminate intermediaries and reduce transaction costs.

Built on platforms like Ethereum and Binance Smart Chain.

Writing a Smart Contract with Solidity

Solidity is the most popular language for writing smart contracts on the **Ethereum blockchain**.

Install   **Solidity**:
You'll need tools like **Remix IDE** or a local development environment with **Truffle** or **Hardhat** for Solidity.

Write a Smart Contract

```solidity
// SPDX-License-Identifier: MIT
pragma solidity ^0.8.0;
```

```
contract SimpleStorage {
    uint256 storedData;

    function set(uint256 x) public {
        storedData = x;
    }

    function get() public view returns (uint256)
{

        return storedData;
    }
}
```

Deploy the Smart Contract
Deploy it using **Remix IDE** or **Truffle** to the **Ethereum network**.

Decentralized Application (DApp)

A **DApp** is a decentralized application that interacts with a blockchain via **smart contracts**.

Frontend (React + Web3.js) for DApp
Build the frontend of the DApp using **React** and **Web3.js** to interact with Ethereum's smart contracts.

```
sh
```

```
npm install web3
```

Simple Web3.js Example to Call a Smart Contract

```
javascript
```

```javascript
const Web3 = require('web3');
const              web3           =            new
Web3('https://mainnet.infura.io/v3/YOUR_INFURA_
PROJECT_ID');

const contractABI = [...];  // ABI from Remix or
Truffle
const contractAddress = '0xYourContractAddress';
const          myContract          =            new
web3.eth.Contract(contractABI, contractAddress);

myContract.methods.get().call()
  .then(result => console.log(result));
```

DApps enable decentralized finance (DeFi), gaming, and more, by providing **secure, trustless interactions** with the blockchain.

Conclusion: Blockchain Applications and Smart Contracts

Key Takeaways

Python and C# are powerful for building blockchain applications.

Smart contracts automate and secure transactions on the blockchain.

DApps are decentralized applications that interact with smart contracts for **trustless** user experiences.

Solidity is the primary language for **Ethereum smart contracts**, and **Web3.js** connects the frontend to the blockchain.

Next Chapter: Serverless Computing and Edge Computing in Cross-Platform Apps

CHAPTER 20

THE FUTURE OF CROSS-PLATFORM DEVELOPMENT

Cross-platform development is rapidly evolving with emerging technologies and frameworks that enable developers to build **faster, more efficient, and scalable applications** across various platforms. In this chapter, we'll explore:

Where Python, C#, and .NET Core are Headed

Emerging Frameworks & Technologies

Final Thoughts and Career Opportunities

Where Python, C#, and .NET Core Are Headed

The Future of Python in Cross-Platform Development

Python's popularity continues to rise, and its role in **cross-platform development** will only grow. With its extensive

libraries and **frameworks**, Python is set to be a key player in **AI, machine learning, and data science** on all platforms.

Key Developments for Python

- **Python 3.10 & Beyond**: New language features like **pattern matching** and **improved performance** are enhancing Python's capabilities for scalable, production-level applications.
- **Mobile Development**: Frameworks like **Kivy** and **BeeWare** are enabling Python developers to build mobile apps for **Android and iOS**.
- **WebAssembly**: Python's future with **WebAssembly** opens the door for **high-performance web applications** written in Python.
- **PyScript**: The upcoming **PyScript** project will allow Python to run directly in the browser, further expanding its reach for web apps.

Predictions for Python

- **Increased Focus on AI/ML**: Python is already the go-to language for AI and machine learning, and with frameworks like **TensorFlow** and **PyTorch**, its role in **intelligent applications** will continue to grow.

- **Enhanced Cross-Platform Frameworks**: Python's **cross-platform reach** will only expand with tools like **PyInstaller** for packaging and **Qt** for UI development.

The Future of C# in Cross-Platform Development

C# and the **.NET ecosystem** continue to evolve as a **top choice** for developing **cross-platform** applications. With **.NET 6** and **.NET 7**, Microsoft is pushing to make C# and **.NET Core** even more powerful and flexible across platforms.

Key Developments for C# & .NET Core

- **.NET MAUI**: The evolution of **Xamarin**, .NET MAUI is set to become the **go-to framework** for building **cross-platform apps** for **Android, iOS, macOS**, and **Windows** with a single codebase.
- **Cross-Platform Backend**: The **ASP.NET Core** framework is widely used for building **cross-platform web apps** and APIs, enabling **scalable backends** with **Docker** and **Kubernetes**.
- **Blazor**: With **Blazor WebAssembly**, C# developers can now build **interactive web UIs** using C# instead of JavaScript.

214

Predictions for C# & .NET Core

- **Unification of Platforms**: **.NET MAUI** will unify desktop, mobile, and web apps under one framework, making C# development more streamlined.
- **Cloud-Native and Microservices**: C# and **.NET Core** are increasingly being adopted for **cloud-native** development, with strong support for **microservices**, **containerization**, and **serverless computing**.
- **WebAssembly in .NET**: With **Blazor**, C# developers will be able to build **WebAssembly-powered apps**, bringing C# to the web like never before.

Emerging Frameworks & Technologies

As cross-platform development continues to grow, new **frameworks and technologies** are constantly emerging to support a wide range of use cases.

New Cross-Platform Frameworks

Flutter (Dart)

- **Flutter** is rapidly growing in the mobile development world, allowing developers to build **natively compiled**

applications from a single codebase for **Android, iOS, Web, and desktop**.

- **Flutter's declarative UI framework** makes it easy to develop complex, highly responsive user interfaces with rich animations.

React Native (JavaScript)

- **React Native** continues to be a strong contender in mobile app development, offering developers the ability to write **cross-platform apps** using **JavaScript** and **React**.
- The community is also pushing **React Native for Windows** and **macOS**, bringing **cross-platform capabilities** beyond just mobile.

Rust and WebAssembly

- **Rust** is gaining popularity for **high-performance** cross-platform development, with its **memory safety** features making it ideal for **systems programming**.
- **WebAssembly** allows languages like **Rust** and **C#** to run **natively** in the browser, opening up a new realm for cross-platform web apps.

Emerging Technologies in Cross-Platform Development

Edge Computing

- **Edge computing** is the next frontier for cross-platform development, enabling data processing and computation closer to the data source (e.g., on IoT devices). Technologies like **Azure IoT Edge** and **AWS IoT Greengrass** are making it easier to manage cross-platform applications at the edge.

5G and IoT

- The advent of **5G networks** will significantly impact mobile development, enabling **real-time data transfer** and **enhanced IoT integration**.
- Cross-platform frameworks will need to evolve to handle the complexities of **low-latency communication** and **increased device connectivity**.

Final Thoughts and Career Opportunities

Final Thoughts on Cross-Platform Development

Cross-platform development continues to be a **key trend** in modern software engineering. Whether you're using **Python** for its flexibility and simplicity, or **C#/.NET Core** for its performance and enterprise support, there is a **huge demand** for developers skilled in creating applications that work seamlessly across multiple platforms.

Core Skills for Cross-Platform Developers

- **Familiarity with multiple platforms** (e.g., Android, iOS, Windows, macOS, Linux)
- **Experience with cross-platform frameworks** (e.g., .NET MAUI, Xamarin, Flutter, React Native, Kivy)
- **Cloud and serverless architecture knowledge** (AWS, Azure, Kubernetes)
- **Proficiency in C#, Python, and web development languages** (JavaScript, HTML, CSS)

Career Opportunities in Cross-Platform Development

Cross-platform developers are in high demand across industries such as **mobile development**, **IoT**, **game development**, and **enterprise applications**. Some potential career paths include:

1. Mobile App Developer

Develop mobile applications using **Flutter**, **React Native**, or **.NET MAUI** to target multiple platforms with a single codebase.

2. IoT Engineer

Work with **Raspberry Pi**, **Arduino**, and other IoT platforms to build connected devices, from home automation systems to industrial IoT solutions.

3. Full-Stack Developer

Build web applications using **React**, **Angular**, or **Blazor** and backends with **ASP.NET Core** or **Python** to support cross-platform, cloud-native applications.

4. Cloud Architect

Design and implement **cloud-based architectures** that support cross-platform applications, including serverless, containerized, and microservices-based systems.

5. Blockchain Developer

Build decentralized applications (DApps) and smart contracts using **Python**, **Solidity**, or **C#** to integrate with blockchain platforms.

6. Game Developer

Use **Unity** (C#) or **Godot** (C# or GDScript) for cross-platform game development across **PC, consoles, mobile devices, and the web**.

Conclusion: A Bright Future for Cross-Platform Development

Cross-platform development is not just about building apps for different platforms—it's about **creating seamless user experiences**, **maximizing efficiency**, and **future-proofing your skills**. The world of cross-platform development is full of exciting challenges and **endless opportunities**.

Next Chapter: Advanced Cross-Platform Architectures and Design Patterns